Enduring Storms

A Mission 119 Guide to James

Hutson Smelley

Enduring Storms

Unless otherwise indicated, Bible quotations are taken from The King James Bible.

ISBN: 978-0-9861336-6-4

www.proclaimtheword.me

Other Works by the Author

Better with Jesus: A Mission 119 Guide to Hebrews (2015)

Love, Romance and Intimacy: A Mission 119 Guide to the
Song of Solomon (2016)

Chasing Jonah: A Mission 119 Guide to Jonah (2018)

Deconstructing Calvinism - Third Edition (2019)

Living Hope: A Mission 119 Guide to First Peter (2019)

Looking Forward, Living Now: A Mission 119 Guide to
Zechariah (2020)

Table of Contents

Preface to the Mission 119 Series

The psalmist declares, "Thy word is a lamp unto my feet, and a light unto my path." (Psalm 119:105) The Bible is unlike all other books, not only in its grandeur and scope, but because its words are God's Words. The Bible presents to us God's special revelation of Himself, His biased view of history past and future, the reality of who we are, and a picture of all that we can be. Woven within its pages and spilling over is God's redemptive plan for humanity, with Jesus Christ as centerpiece. We do not study the Bible merely to accumulate head knowledge, but with the earnest expectation of knowing God more and drawing near to Him. Each page has something for us, sometimes encouraging us, sometimes reproving us, always revealing God, and every jot and tittle a precious morsel for our souls. Against the backdrop of a world in darkness, it is the light of truth that pierces through all the deceptions and puts reality in clear focus.

Every generation faces challenges, and the present generation is challenged about truth and whether any absolute truths are knowable. Like all the ones before it, this generation needs to hear God's Word taught boldly, with clarity, without apology, in grace and love. And this generation needs to be reminded by those who teach that the Bible was written for everyone. God has spoken with clarity so that all believers who come to the Bible yielded to what God has for them can know its truths as they grow and mature. The aim here is to strike the proper balance between too little detail to elucidate the message and superfluous detail that obscures, so that this volume is accessible and profitable to laypersons and teachers alike who seek to understand the author's original intended meaning and the continuing relevance of that message today. With this in mind, the Mission 119 Series is designed to provide guidance for the exposition of books of the Bible with depth and a commitment to a plain sense interpretation tethered first and foremost to the context and flow of argument of the book under consideration before comparison is made to other books and the perceived systematic theology of the Bible. Of a certainty, the Bible has one author and contains neither error nor contradiction, but each of the 66 books and letters in the Bible must be allowed first to speak for itself as the teacher helps learners see the message of the book in context and its application principles.

A common sentiment today is that people need only "relevant" teaching from the Bible, which suggests portions of the Bible are irrelevant, and too often means they want three steps to raising teens in place of the perfections of God, five steps to a better marriage in place of how a believer matures and walks in the Spirit, how to find blessing and wealth in place of God's demand for holy living, and so forth. May I say that every word God ever spoke was relevant and remains so today. Those who would step forward as teachers of the Word of God only do people a disservice by trying to conform God's Holy Word to the world's bankrupt self-help counterfeits when what is most needful today is the plain teaching of the whole Bible as it is. Believers engaged in the Word and yielding to the Holy Spirit will find the most practical of wisdom and grace enablement for all areas of their lives as they draw near to God in the transformative experience of knowing Him more and more. May I also suggest that while some people will flee teaching that has depth and conviction, far more people in churches today are thirsty for more depth in the teaching. They want to see that the Bible is not clichés and recycled sugar sticks but truly a light from God unto their paths. In this vein, it is my prayer that this volume of the Mission 119 Series will be a useful guide for teachers of the Bible and a special blessing for students of the Word who aspire to know God more.

Chapter 1

Introductory Matters

The epistle of James may best be described as a primer on Christian living. The book extols the Lord Jesus's command that we love others, and the reader cannot help but see James' love for his readers and concern for their well-being. He writes much as a pastor who knows exactly where his readers are in their Christian experience and speaks in practical terms to their most pressing spiritual needs. The book is theologically rich, addressing such matters as a divine perspective on trials, growing to spiritual maturity, and the relationship between the Christian walk and the coming works judgment.

The modern reader will find that James' epistle is just as relevant and applicable today as it was for its original audience. Our core struggles remain the same as these early Christians. We don't understand trials from God's perspective. We acknowledge Jesus' command to love others but fail to see what that means when it comes to how we speak and act toward others in various situations. The center of our difficulties is our pride, our inability to handle conflicts with others, and our need for God's grace enablement. All of that is powerfully and practically addressed in the book of James. I agree with Adamson: "With few exceptions, we are sure, there is nothing in the Epistle of James that is not thoroughly applicable and relevant to today."[1]

A Misunderstood Book

Unfortunately, for most Christians the book of James is a missed blessing. James is among the easiest New Testament epistles to interpret and almost certainly the most misunderstood in the New Testament. The book suffers from a long history of exegetical confusion going back to Augustine, who introduced the idea that the book is a warning to false converts with fake faith in the gospel of Christ as demonstrated by their lack of Christian works. This misunderstanding, centered on James 2:14-26, overshadows the entire epistle as the lens through which most readers understand the book. But this error is not due to difficult and questionable verses like the "warning" passages in Hebrews or the symbolic imagery in the Revelation. Rather, a relentless theological blindness leads people to insist on what the epistle means despite all indications to the contrary within the text. Worse still, the eisogesis of James spills over to other New Testament writings and has been used to cut from whole cloth a systematic theology about fake faith in Christ. But James is nothing if not plainspoken, and if his concern was that his readers believed they were Christians but were on their way to hell, he would have said so explicitly and made a point of presenting a complete gospel presentation.

---

[1] James B. Adamson, *The Epistle of James*, The New International Commentary on the New Testament (Grand Rapids, MI: Wm. B. Eerdmans Publishing Co., 1976), 21.

The failure to rightly understand this epistle stems from two primary hermeneutical errors. First, too many have failed to appreciate and give proper weight to the organization and structure of the book. Disputed verses like James 2:14 are read in isolation rather than in the context of the unit of thought within which they occur. Most commentaries make little effort to relate their view of James 2:14 to the judgment of James 2:12-13 or the larger unit of thought that begins in James 1:21. Second, key words are assigned meanings to fit a theological commitment, which results in circular reasoning. It is impossible to correctly exegete Bible verses if we implant our preconceived theology into them by mis-defining the key words. While we are entitled to our own opinions, we are not entitled to our own definitions. The most obvious theological seeding of the text is how many commentators insist without credible evidence that the content of the "faith" in James 2:14 is the gospel of Christ and the salvation in view is deliverance from the penalty of sin or deliverance from hell. Everything about James' words rejects these interpretations. Accordingly, as we undertake this study, I will place a heavy emphasis on the organizational structure of the book and the meanings of key terms in the context in which James employs them.

Author of the Book

As Moyter points out, the "long-standing tradition attributes the letter to James the Lord's brother. It was not until the sixteenth century that this attribution was disputed..."[2] Grant Osborne similarly writes that "the

---

[2] J. A. Motyer, *The Message of James: The Tests of Faith*, The Bible Speaks Today (Leicester, England; Downers Grove, IL: Inter-Varsity Press, 1985), 18.

church has consistently held to authorship by James the Lord's brother for most of its history, and the evidence of the epistle itself supports that thesis."[3] Thomas Lea states that "[t]he early church also accepted the Lord's half brother as the author of the writing."[4]

While the mere use of the common name "James" in the epistle does not necessitate that the author "be identified with a James mentioned in the New Testament... the use of the name by itself in a letter written with such authority implies that the author was a well-known figure and it is improbable that such an individual would have gone unmentioned in the New Testament."[5] There are four people named James referenced in the New Testament: (1) James the father of Judas (Luke 6:16), (2) James the son of Alphaeus (Mark 3:18), (3) James the son of Zebedee and brother of John (Acts 12:2), and (4) James the Lord's brother (Mark 6:3; Acts 15:13).[6] The first two possibilities are highly improbable as they were not well known. As Moo explains of James the brother of John: "James the son of Zebedee, however, died a martyr's death in AD 44 (Acts 12:2) and it is unlikely that the epistle was written as early as this. We are left, therefore, with James, the Lord's brother, as the most likely author of the

---

3 Grant R. Osborne, "James," in *Cornerstone Biblical Commentary: James, 1–2 Peter, Jude, Revelation*, ed. Philip W. Comfort, Cornerstone Biblical Commentary (Carol Stream, IL: Tyndale House Publishers, 2011), 4.

4 Thomas D. Lea, *Hebrews, James*, vol. 10, Holman New Testament Commentary (Nashville, TN: Broadman & Holman Publishers, 1999), 251.

5 Douglas J. Moo, *James: An Introduction and Commentary*, vol. 16, Tyndale New Testament Commentaries (Downers Grove, IL: InterVarsity Press, 1985), 20.

6 Thomas D. Lea, *Hebrews, James*, 251.

epistle."[7] But more can be said in favor of James the Lord's brother as the author. At several places in the epistle James shows a first-hand familiarity with Jesus' teachings.[8] In particular, as Fruchtenbaum states, "[t]here are a number of similarities between what Jacob/James writes and what Jesus said at the Sermon on the Mount."[9] I concur with Kurt Richardson that "[t]he cumulative evidence points clearly to James the brother of Jesus as the author of this epistle."[10]

James the Lord's Brother

We know a good deal about James from several references to him in the New Testament. We know that Jesus had at least six younger siblings, and among them was James. (Matthew 13:55-56) James did not come to faith in Jesus as the Christ until after the resurrection. (1 Corinthians 15:7) After that, he quickly took on a leadership role in the local church in Jerusalem. This is evident because when Peter was released from prison in Acts 12, he went to the family home of Mark and his mother and said to those who were gathered there praying, "Go shew these things unto James, and to the brethren. And he departed, and went into another place." (Acts 12:17) As Grant Osborne explains: "Then at the critical Jerusalem Council in Acts 15:13–21, it is his final speech that turns the tide and enables the church to accept that the Gentile mission is

---

[7] Douglas J. Moo, *James*, 20.

[8] Thomas D. Lea, *Hebrews, James*, 251.

[9] Arnold G. Fruchtenbaum, *Hebrews, James, I & II Peter, Jude: Exposition from a Messianic Jewish Perspective* (Tustin, CA: Ariel Ministries, 2005), 215.

[10] Kurt A. Richardson, *James*, vol. 36, The New American Commentary (Nashville: Broadman & Holman Publishers, 1997), 41.

God's will. Then in the 'Jerusalem decree' of Acts 15:22–29, James and the other leaders asked the Gentile converts to respect certain Jewish sensitivities. In both instances James was a central figure in the Jerusalem church, in a sense acting as its head elder."[11] We also read in Acts 21:18-19 that the apostle Paul meets with James and other elders in Jerusalem. Moo provides a good summary of James' reputation and martyrdom:

> This James became a popular and respected figure in the early church, especially among Jewish Christians. He was venerated as the first 'bishop' of Jerusalem and was given the title 'the righteous' or 'the just' because of his faithfulness to the law and constancy in prayer. Much of our information about James comes from Hegesippus' account of James' death as recorded by Eusebius (*H.E.* II.23). He tells us that James was stoned by the scribes and Pharisees for refusing to renounce his commitment to Jesus. This account of James' death is independently confirmed by Josephus (*Ant.* XX.9.1), who also enables us to date it in AD 62.[12]

Date and Audience

Given James' martyrdom in AD 62, his epistle must have been written before then. Because there is no reference to any Gentile controversy regarding Jewish law, the epistle was likely written very early when the Church was still predominantly Jewish, and prior to the Jerusalem Council

---

[11] Grant R. Osborne, "James," 4.
[12] Douglas J. Moo, *James*, 20–21.

of Acts 15 (AD 49). Most conservative scholars date the book between A.D. 45 and 50.[13] But some argue for a date as early as AD 34 or 35:

> If the traditional date of James's death (A.D. 62) is correct, the epistle cannot have been written later than that. Instead, the absence of any concern with the issues raised by the conversion of Gentiles, suggests the possibility that the letter might be dated as early as the middle or late 30s. We may take April 3, A.D. 33 as the date of the crucifixion. (For a convincing discussion, see Maier, *ChHist* 3–13.) The conversion of Saul of Tarsus (Paul) could have taken place in A.D. 34, leaving about a year, or a little more, for the events of Acts 1–9. In that case James could plausibly be dated as early as A.D. 34. As Robinson has noted (*Redating*, p. 121), "there is nothing in James that goes outside what is described in the first half of Acts." We may add that nothing in the epistle goes beyond Acts 1–9.[14]

James identifies his audience as "the twelve tribes which are scattered abroad." (James 1:1) The book was written to Jewish believers of the dispersion, which "may refer to the general dispersion or it might refer specifically to the dispersion of Jewish believers resulting from the stoning

---

[13] Fruchtenbaum, *Hebrews, James, I & II Peter, Jude: Exposition from a Messianic Jewish Perspective*, 212.

[14] Zane C. Hodges, Arthur L. Farstad, and Robert N. Wilkin, *The Epistle of James: Proven Character through Testing* (Irving, TX: Grace Evangelical Society, 1994), 10.

of Stephen (Acts 8;1, 4; 11:19-20)."[15] It is likely that the scattered Jewish Christian readers are outside of Israel and composed of those scattered as a result of persecution in Israel as well as those converted in the dispersion.[16]

Purpose and Outline

The primary purpose of James is to encourage his readers to faithfulness to God's Word (especially the command to love others) in the midst of their trials, to explain how God uses trials to develop endurance and grow them to maturity, and to explain the nature of the coming judgment of their works before the Lord Jesus Christ. Below is an outline of the epistle of James:

I.   GREETING (1:1)

II. GOD USES TESTS AND TRIALS TO GROW US TO MATURITY (1:1-18)

    a. Trials produce endurance leading to maturity (1:2-4)

    b. Trials produce wisdom (1:5-11)

    c. Trials produce happiness (1:12-18)

        i.   Trials lead to receiving the crown of life (1:12)

        ii. Don't blame God when you sin and experience death (1:13-15)

        iii. God gives good gifts, including eternal salvation (1:16-18)

---

[15] Fruchtenbaum, *Hebrews, James, I & II Peter, Jude*, 212.
[16] Grant R. Osborne, "James," 6–7.

III. <u>**CENTRAL EXHORTATION:**</u> THE CHRISTIAN GROWING TO MATURITY IS QUICK TO HEAR, SLOW TO SPEAK AND SLOW TO ANGER (1:19-20)

IV. GOOD HEARERS HUMBLY EMBRACE GOD'S IMPLANTED WORD AND LIVE IT OUT TO THE SAVING OF THE SOUL-LIFE AT THE JUDGMENT (1:21-2:26)

    a. <u>**Key Principle About Being Swift to Hear**</u>: Putting aside sin and humbly embracing God's Word can save your soul-life (1:21)

    b. Knowing God's Word does is not the same as embracing and experiencing His Word (1:22-27)

        i. The attitude toward God's Word of someone who does not embrace it and apply it to life (1:23-24)

        ii. The attitude toward God's Word of someone who embraces it and applies the law of liberty to life (1:25)

        iii. The empty religion and self-deception of the person who does not embrace God's Word is revealed by his or her uncontrolled speech (1:26)

        iv. The authentic religion of the person who does embrace God's Word is revealed by his or her application of the law of liberty to life (1:27)

    c. Our obedience to the law of liberty (royal law) will be approved at the judgment and save our soul-life (2:1-26)

i. A practical example – showing favoritism in the church based on wealth violates the law of liberty (royal law) (2:1-7)

   1. Favoring the wealthy reveals sinful motives (2:1-4)

   2. Favoring the wealthy ignores that it is the poor in the world that will inherit in the kingdom (2:5-7)

ii. Fulfilling the royal law will find approval at the judgment (2:8-13)

   1. The royal law is to love others (2:8)

   2. Favoritism violates the royal law and makes one a transgressor (2:9-11)

   3. The law of liberty is the standard applied at the judgment to our speech and actions (2:12-13)

iii. Knowing and believing God's Word without also living it out will not profit us at the judgment (2:14-26)

   1. The first faith-works <u>inclusio</u>: a faith without works will not save your soul-life at the judgment (2:14-17)

   2. The diatribe against the hypothetical objector (2:18-19)

   3. The second faith-works <u>inclusio</u>: a faith without works is useless (2:20-26)

V. BE SLOW TO SPEAK BECAUSE YOUR WORDS WILL BE JUDGED AND HOW YOU SPEAK REVEALS YOUR MATURITY AND THE WISDOM YOU LIVE BY (3:1-18)

a. <u>**Key Principle About Being Slow to Speak**</u>: Be wise about becoming a teacher of God's Word because you will be subject to a stricter judgment. (3:1)

b. Controlling our speech is a hallmark of spiritual maturity and indicates disciplined control over our entire body (works). (3:2-4)

   i. Illustrated by the use of a small bit to control the entire horse's body. (3:3)

   ii. Illustrated by the use of a small rudder to control the entire ship. (3:4)

   iii. Negatively illustrated by a small fire the scorches an entire forest. (3:5)

   iv. Lack of control of our speech will pollute our entire body (works). (3:6)

c. Our speech cannot be completely controlled. (3:7-12)

   i. Contrasted with animals that can be tamed. (3:7)

   ii. Our speech cannot be completely controlled because it is corrupted. (3:8-10)

   iii. The incongruity of uncontrolled speech illustrated by a spring of water, a fig tree, and a grape vine. (3:11-12)

d. Our speech is a reflection of the wisdom we choose to live by. (3:13-18)

    i. Our Christian works show we are living in humility that derives from heavenly wisdom. (3:13)

    ii. But boasting and lying shows selfish ambition in our hearts that derives from worldly, demonic wisdom. (3:14-16)

    iii. Heavenly wisdom lived out produces godly thinking and the fruit of righteousness and peace with one another. (3:17-18)

VI. BE SLOW TO WRATH / ANGER (4:1-5:6)

  a. **<u>Key Principle About Being Slow to Wrath</u>**: Your worldliness causes strife with other Christians and hostility toward God. (4:1-5)

    i. Worldliness causes strife with other Christians. (4:1-2)

    ii. Worldliness ruins your prayer life. (4:2-3)

    iii. A love affair with the world creates hostility with God. (4:4-5)

  b. Humble submission to God prevents the negative results of worldliness. (4:6-5:6).

    i. Humility brings us closer to God and He exalts us. (4:6-10)

      1. God gives grace to the humble. (4:6)

      2. Submit to God and resist the devil. (4:7)

      3. Draw near to God with clean hands and pure hearts. (4:8)

      4. Mourn and weep over your sin. (4:9)

5. Humble yourself before God and He will exalt you. (4:10)

ii. Humility prevents critical speech toward fellow Christians. (4:11-12)

   1. Critical speech toward fellow Christians makes us judges of the royal law rather than doers of the royal law. (4:11)

   2. Only God has the right to judge. (4:12)

iii. Humility prevents us from leaving God out of our plans. (4:13-17)

   1. Illustrated by arrogant speech (plans) that leaves God out. (4:13)

   2. Humility recognizes that we are not guaranteed tomorrow. (4:14)

   3. Our speech (plans) should reflect our submission to God. (4:15)

   4. Boastful speech (plans) is sin. (4:16-17)

iv. Humility prevents us from acting like the wicked rich people who will be judged for oppressing the poor. (5:1-6)

   1. The rich oppressors are called upon to mourn their coming judgment. (5:1)

   2. Their ill-gotten wealth will stand witness against them. (5:2-4)

   3. They lived out worldly desires fattening their hearts for the coming judgment. (5:5)

   4. They murdered the righteous who did not resist. (5:6)

VII. CLOSING EXHORTATIONS TO ENDURE IN TRIALS KNOWING THE LORD'S RETURN IS NEAR (5:7-11)

a. Be patient and strengthen your hearts in the knowledge that the Lord's return is near. (5:7-8)

b. Don't fight with fellow Christians because the judge will soon return. (5:9)

c. Illustrated by the prophets who endured through suffering. (5:10)

d. Illustrated by the life of Job, which also shows the Lord's mercy. (5:11)

VIII. CLOSING EXHORTATIONS ON SPEECH (5:12-20)

a. Don't take oaths, but tell the truth. (5:12)

b. The suffering should pray and the merry should sing praises. (5:13)

c. The church elders should anoint and pray over the spiritually weary. (5:14-15)

d. Pray for one another knowing the effectiveness of the prayer of a righteous person. (5:16)

e. Illustrated in the prayers of Elijah. (5:17-18)

f. Share the truth to Christians caught up in false doctrine. (5:19-20)

Chapter 2

Trials Can Grow Us to Maturity

James 1:1-18

To know the Bible well is much more than knowing what it says. Because we cannot do what we do not know, the information in the Bible is necessary and critical to our Christian walk. But we never truly know the Bible until it is experientially learned.

Imagine reading a car repair manual. Even if you could master the book, your knowledge is academic and untested unless and until you successfully perform actual automotive repairs. A good mechanic knows the information in the manual, but he or she is only a good mechanic because he or she has experience diagnosing automotive problems and repairing them. Being a good mechanic is experientially learned, and not everyone that has read a repair manual is a good mechanic. Not only that, the "mechanic" that knows the manual but never gets past checking the oil level and tire pressure is not a good mechanic. To be a good mechanic, you have to get your hands dirty with increasingly challenging tasks from brake jobs to opening the engine up to rebuild it. Learning the Bible for real life change looks much the same and you have to know the manual and get your hands dirty.

The Bible claims for itself to contain information that can radically change our lives. Paul wrote that the Bible is "profitable for doctrine, for reproof, for correction, for instruction in righteousness." (2 Timothy 3:16) But no matter how well we know what the words on the pages say, that alone does not equate to righteousness. It is taking God's Word and applying it faithfully in our daily lives that makes us good mechanics of righteousness. (Hebrews 5:13) We deal with all kinds of issues and decisions every day of our lives. Some of these issues and decisions are routine—like checking the oil level and tire pressure in a car. It is important that these routine issues are faithfully handled on the basis of God's Word, but they will not make us skilled at life. It is the non-routine challenges of life—what we might call tests and trials— that if faithfully handled on the basis of God's Word will develop us into master mechanics of righteousness.

Outline

I. GREETING (1:1)

II. GOD USES TESTS AND TRIALS TO GROW US TO MATURITY (1:1-18)

    a. Trials produce endurance leading to maturity (1:2-4)

    b. Trials produce wisdom (1:5-11)

c. Trials produce happiness (1:12-18)

    i. Trials lead to receiving the crown of life (1:12)

    ii. Don't blame God when you sin and experience death (1:13-15)

    iii. God gives good gifts, including eternal salvation (1:16-18)

Scripture and Comments

James writes to an audience of primarily Jewish Christians that know something about God's Word but are a long way from being righteous in their daily experience. He knows many of them are facing varying degrees of trials and that it is those trials that can help them develop their experiential knowledge of the Word and grow them to maturity. His letter to them, written with a pastor's heart, opens right where they are at, in the middle of difficulties and needing a divine perspective of their current experience and exhortations to practical Christian living.

> **James 1:1** James, a servant of God and of the Lord Jesus Christ, to the twelve tribes which are scattered abroad, greeting.

Typical of first century Jewish letters, the epistle begins by identifying the author and greeting the recipients. The author identifies himself as **James, a servant of God and of the Lord Jesus Christ**. As I covered in the introductory materials, the author is **James**, the half-brother of **Jesus**. We know **James** sometimes traveled with **Jesus** during his earthly ministry (see, e.g., Matthew 12:46; John 2:12), and as a consequence he no doubt personally heard much of **Jesus'** teaching. Much of what **James** has for us is reflected in **Jesus'** teachings recorded in the Gospels.

While **James** might have self-promoted by adding that he is **Jesus'** half-brother, he does not do so. Even in his brief salutation, there is a lesson for us. **James** identifies as **a servant**. The Greek word translated **servant** is δοῦλος (doulos). The notes to the NET Bible explain: "Though δοῦλος (doulos) is normally translated 'servant,' the word does not bear the connotation of a free individual serving another." The Greek lexicon BDAG defines the term as a "male slave as an entity in a socioeconomic context." It further notes that the translation "'servant' for 'slave' is largely confined to Biblical [translations] and early American times...in normal usage at the present time the two words are carefully distinguished." In short, **James** sees himself as a slave. There were self-promoting Christian leaders in the first century. (see Philippians 1:15-17) There are many today as well. Many nationally known preachers and "televangelists" are multimillionaires through their successful self-promotion. Still other teachers and leaders are not guilty of this type of self-promotion, but they are bubbling with pride, which is evident in how they talk about those with whom they disagree. And we must ask, would they align with **James** as a slave **of God and of the Lord Jesus Christ**? But we must take the extra step and make it personal. Will I be a slave **of God and of the Lord Jesus Christ**?

To be a slave is a position of humility and devoted service. Some religions promise earthly greatness. Christianity offers the blessing of humble service to **Jesus Christ** and putting the needs of others first. From the outset, this epistle emphasizes living for **Jesus**. James exhorts his audience to "be ye doers of the word, and not hearers only." (James 1:22) A **servant** will always be a doer of his Lord's commands.

He writes **to the twelve tribes which are scattered abroad**. The term translated **scattered abroad** is the Greek διασπορά (*diaspora*), which came to be a technical term referring to Jewish people residing in Gentile nations. As recorded in the Old Testament, many Jewish people of the Northern Kingdom (Samaria) were removed from the land by the Assyrians in the 8th century B.C., and then many Jewish people of the Southern Kingdom (Judah) were removed from the land by the Babylonians in the 6th century B.C. The latter were subjected to 70 years of bondage just as Jeremiah prophesied, and after they were permitted to return home, most did not. This continued into the first century with many Jewish people establishing new lives for their families outside of Israel. However, religious Jews would pilgrimage to Jerusalem for some of the feasts, as we see in Act 2 regarding Pentecost. The audience that heard Peter's sermon in Acts 2 was primarily Jewish with some Gentile proselytes, and many of them traveled to Jerusalem for the feast from other nations, i.e., from the diaspora. After Acts 2, many of them returned to their home nations in the diaspora. It is also likely that James' audience includes early Jewish Christians who fled the persecution that began in Jerusalem with the martyrdom of Stephen in Acts 7. As David Anderson explains, "These people are Jewish Christians who, like seed from the sower, were sown throughout the world of that day as the cycle of persecution swept through early Christendom."[17]

James writes to the Jewish believers **scattered abroad** in the Gentile nations. To them he sends his **greeting**. The word **greeting** is the Greek χαίρω (chairō) and is much

---

[17] David R. Anderson, *Triumph through Trials: The Epistle of James* (Grace Theology Press, 2013), 5.

more than a "hello" that we might expect. The word means to be cheerful or rejoice. If we were put to finding a single word that would describe the essence of this epistle, the word "rejoice" would do well. **James** writes to people that generally know persecution first-hand and right out of the gate he tells them to rejoice. The prologue that follows in vv. 2-18 explains the divine perspective that permits, and even objectively compels, rejoicing in the storms they (and we) face.

> **James 1:2** My brethren, count it all joy when ye fall into divers temptations; **3** Knowing *this*, that the trying of your faith worketh patience. **4** But let patience have *her* perfect work, that ye may be perfect and entire, wanting nothing.

As his epistle will bear out, James' primary concern is proper Christian living and spiritual growth to maturity. He repeatedly addresses his audience as **brethren**. But unfortunately, this epistle has been hijacked by those with a theological commitment that James necessarily addresses a mixed audience of genuine believers and self-deceived people who think and profess they are Christians but are not. They have fake or so-called "spurious" faith. This eisogesis has a long history back to Augustine, and centers in how people handle James 2:14-26. The key to properly interpreting James, as with all of the New Testament epistles, is starting at the beginning of the book—not in the middle—with careful exegesis that seeks to determine not just meanings of words, phrases and verses, but the structure of the epistle and the core argument(s) of the book. The epistle is highly structured as the proposed outline shows. The prologue (vv. 2-18) is critical to our understanding of the book because it introduces core issues that relate to how we daily live as Christians, not how we become Christians. As I commented in the prior chapter, James is a straightforward epistle that has been made confusing and difficult by an unrelenting willful bias.

James' greeting tells his audience to rejoice, which might have left his audience scratching their heads. But he doubles down in these verses, telling them to **count it all joy** when they face trials. He does not offer empty optimism like "find the silver lining in your trials" or "keep your head up." He says **count it all**, i.e., complete, total, 100%, **joy**. These words introduce a new perspective on trials that is contrary to our flesh and conventional (or worldly) wisdom. We prefer smooth waters, good health, strong relationships, and consistent employment. We do not like storms, illnesses and personal conflict. Yet James says **count it all joy**. We cannot write this off as pious platitude because "God is in control." Of course He is in control, but there is more here. James opens his letter with these powerful, and perhaps disquieting, words to get his audience's attention and focus them on a divine perspective about what they were experiencing. I would suggest that for a mature Christian there is nothing curious about what James says, but for a new or immature believer, his words are provocative and unsettling. Probably he intended that.

There are key terms we must analyze to put together what James is saying. Good exegesis involves picking up each rock (words, phrases) and examining it carefully. Key terms here include **brethren, count, all joy, when, diverse, temptations, knowing, trying, faith, worketh, patience**, and **perfect**. Note again that James refers to his audience as **my brethren**. The Greek word translated **brethren** may be used to refer to brothers and sisters, and in this context, as the NET translation notes explain, **brethren** means fellow Christians. James explicitly refers to their eternal salvation in 1:18. James refers to his audience 19 times as **brethren**, speaking to his audience as Christians and not a mixed group. His primary message about spiritual growth would hardly be appropriate to non-Christians, and nowhere in the book does James address the complete content of the gospel of Christ. James assumes a regenerate audience and addresses the common needs they have, which center on spiritual growth and trials. As Hodges writes: "It may be said that nowhere in the letter—not even in 2:14–26!—does he betray the slightest doubt that those in his audience are truly his brothers or sisters in the Lord. If we do not observe this simple and obvious fact, we may fall into a quagmire of skewed interpretations, just as so many expositors of James have actually done."[18]

To his **brethren** in the dispersion, **James** says, **count it all joy when ye fall into divers temptations.** That he says **when** and not "if" means the **temptations** are to be expected. The word **temptations** is the Greek πειρασμός (peirasmos). BDAG provides two definitions: (1) "an attempt to learn the nature or character of something, *test, trial*" and (2) "an attempt to make one do something wrong, *temptation, enticement* to sin." The context does not support the idea of an enticement to sin, but of the general tests and trials of life. It makes no sense that James would suggest they **count it all joy** when they are enticed to sin because the New Testament says to flee sin. (e.g., 1 Corinthians 6:18, 10:14; 2 Timothy 2:22) James later says, "Resist the devil, and he will flee from you." (James 4:7)

---

18 Zane C. Hodges, Arthur L. Farstad, and Robert N. Wilkin, *James*, 18.

James has in mind **divers** or various types of tests and trials. The word **divers** is the Greek ποικίλος (*poikilos*) and means "pertaining to existence in various kinds or modes, *diversified, manifold.*" In other words, the tests and trials come in all shapes and sizes. We should not think only of severe trials like a broken marriage or loss of a loved one. Day by day and moment by moment we face all kinds of tests and trials. Dr. Harry Leafe always said that life is a series of pop quizzes with some major exams now and then. The question is on what basis will we deal with those tests and trials. Will we work out the problems of life on the basis of God's Word or worldly wisdom?

James says **when** these tests and trials come, we are to **count it all joy**. Most people associate **joy** with experiencing tranquility in relationships and success in endeavors. For them, **joy** is a feeling. But James says to **count it**, using the Greek ἡγέομαι (*hegeomai*), which means "to engage in an intellectual process, *think, consider, regard.*" James is NOT saying we should feel joyous when bad things happen to us. Regardless of how a particular trial makes us subjectively feel, we can **count it all joy** based on a divine perspective of all of the facts. James speaks to our reasoned or intellectual response. But why is **joy** (Greek χαρά [chara] meaning cheerfulness, delight, gladness) a reasoned response to tests and trials? Because those tests and trials can produce spiritual growth, maturity, wisdom, and a superior experience of life. As Harry Leafe explains: "But why are we to consider it nothing but joy? What is the basis for such a response? It is our knowledge of the relationship between faith, tests of faith, maturity, and our inheritance in Christ."[19]

---

[19] G. Harry Leafe, *Running to Win! A Positive Biblical Approach To Rewards And Inheritance* (Biblical Studies Press 2004, 2d ed.), 25.

Non-Christians also face trials, as Christians do, because we live in a fallen world. But God uses the trials in the lives of His children to grow them. (see also Hebrews 12)

James explains the basis for having **all joy** even in tough times: **knowing this, that the trying of your faith worketh patience.** To grasp this concept we must understand what James means by **trying**, what **faith** he has in mind, and what **patience** is. The Greek word translated **trying** is the noun δοκίμιον (dokimion), which can mean (1) "the process or means of determining the genuineness of something, *testing, means of testing*" or (2) the "genuineness as a result of a test, *genuine, without alloy.*" Thus, James either refers to the process of evaluating the quality of their **faith** or the result or outcome of that evaluation. I contend that it is absurd to think that trials always produce **patience** for the simple reason that we often fail to properly handle trials. Rather, what James is saying is that **faith** that has been evaluated and proven through the trial produces **patience**. It helps to observe the identical phrasing in 1 Peter 1:7, the only other place where the word *dokimion* occurs.

There, Peter says "[t]hat the trial of your faith, being much more precious than of gold that perisheth, though it be tried with fire, might be found unto praise and honour and glory at the appearing of Jesus Christ." The noun *dokimion* is translated "trial" (not **trying** as in James 1:3) and the verb form *dokimazō* is translated "tried." In 1 Peter 1:7, it is the proven character of their faith that is "more precious than of gold." Almost all modern translations use something like "the proven character of your faith" rather than "the trial of your faith" to emphasize that it is not the process but the result that has more value than earthly riches. Peter's metaphor is that the quality of precious metals (like gold) is tried with fire to remove the impurities (the dross) and purify the product to make it more valuable. So also the trials of life prove and refine our faith, as we exhibit faith responses to the trials, and the product of that testing—our faith responses—is much more precious or valuable than of gold that perisheth. Hodges supports this reading: "We suggest the meaning, 'your quality-proven faith,' i.e., 'your unalloyed [pure] faith.' James is referring to the way trial and testing apply 'fire' to our faith, so that it can come through the 'furnace' of trouble cleansed of any dross or impurity from the flesh."[20] Similarly, Leafe explains: "The point to be emphasized is this. It is not the trials that result in endurance. It is not gritting one's teeth and hanging in there through the difficulties of life. It is, like a math test, working the problem successfully – passing the test, not just taking it!"[21]

Accordingly, proven **faith** produces **patience**. But to get our minds around this concept, we need to unpack the key terms **faith** and **patience**. When James says **your faith** he assumes they have **faith**. We live in a time when people speak in spiritual terms and it is not uncommon to hear people speak of "faith" in an ambiguous way—"you just need to have faith" or "my faith is important to me." But **faith** means to trust or place confidence in someone or something. Our **faith** must have content, and context must guide our understanding of what that content is in this passage. We cannot assume the **faith** James has in mind is their belief in the gospel of Christ. As already noted, James writes to fellow Christians, and moreover, it

[20] Zane C. Hodges, Arthur L. Farstad, and Robert N. Wilkin, *James*, 19.
[21] Ibid., 26.

hardly makes sense to suggest that the trials of life will determine the quality of a person's belief in the death, burial and resurrection of Jesus Christ.

It is **faith** in God and His provision—including His Word and His wisdom—in our Christian walk that is at issue. In James 1:6, for example, he speaks of asking "in faith" for the wisdom of God in order to successfully face the trials. In James 1:21, he speaks of receiving "with meekness the engrafted word," and in 1:22 he says to be a doer of the Word and not a hearer only. It goes without saying that if we are ignorant of the Word, we will not do well in the trials of life. When the trials come, our **faith** will be proven if we are relying on God's resources and responding to the trials on the basis of God's Word. Do you trust God to see you through (not around) the trials? Will you respond to the trials on the basis of God's Word, His wisdom and His grace? That is what is in view. It is easy to acknowledge that God said to love others as you love yourself, and quite another thing to love others while you are in the furnace. Dillow well states: "Faith in the sense of an ongoing piety and trust and not just in the sense of the act which procures initial salvation is found throughout the Bible. Faith is not only an initial act; it is also a walk, a way of life for the Christian by which he furthers his sanctification, grows, lives richly, and stands firm."[22] And in James' epistle, which uses the term **faith** fifteen times, the usage is consistently with regard to **faith** in God and His resources in our walk: "What does James refer to when he speaks of 'faith'? Is the initial act in view or the ongoing life of trust, the walk of faith, his subject?

---

[22] Joseph C. Dillow, *Final Destiny: The Future Reign of the Servant Kings, 4th Edition* (Houston, TX: Grace Theology Press, 2018).

Usage in the epistle indicates the latter is his theme."[23] There is zero indication anywhere in the entire epistle that their belief in the gospel is in doubt.

The word translated **patience** is ὑπομονή (hupomonē), which means "the capacity to hold out or bear up in the face of difficulty, *patience, endurance, fortitude, steadfastness, perseverance.*" Leafe explains well that **patience** is "steadfast endurance...[t]he term means 'mental toughness, stick-to-it-iveness.' It is a character quality without which we are unable to successfully run 'the race of life' (cf. Heb. 12:1)."[24] But we err if we fail to associate this steadfast endurance to **faith** in God and His provision, by which we can deal with the tests and trials of life. As Anderson puts it, this steadfast endurance is remaining under God's will for us in the trial:

> But the word for patience in the NT Greek is not *hupomonēn.* It is *macrothumia,* which is a fruit of the Spirit in Galatians 5:22. This word *hupomonēn* is made up of two Greek words: *hupo + moneō.* The first means "under," like a hypodermic needle goes under the skin. The second word means, "to remain." Christian endurance is to "remain under" God's revealed desire for our lives. It is as though He is holding a protective umbrella over us to shield us from the worst effects of our trials. We stop enduring when we step out from under His umbrella to try to handle things on our own or simply to follow the flesh. When we

---

23 Ibid.
24 G. Harry Leafe, *Running to Win!,* 26.

are under His umbrella nothing can harm us eternally. The storms will come but they will not touch us. The most severe hailstorm cannot pummel us; the most devastating tornado cannot funnel us away. And to me, that's what this word *hupomonēn* means: to stay under God's umbrella when the storms come. To trust Him and submit to Him during the most threatening and ominous storms—that is endurance.[25]

So putting together the pieces, our proven **faith** in God and His provision, that is, **faith** that brought us through the test or trial, produces steadfast endurance under God's will for our lives. This perspective is part of the basis for experiencing **joy** in our trials, but there is more. James continues, **but let patience** or steadfast endurance **have her perfect work** or end result, **that you may be perfect and entire, wanting** or lacking **nothing.** The term **perfect** (Greek τέλειος) generally means, according to BDAG, "attaining an end or purpose, complete." When used of people, it pertains "to being mature, *full-grown, mature, adult.*" James says to **let** this work of God in our lives through the trial run its course to completion. We usually want the storm to end five minutes ago, but that is not how we learn God's Word experientially and grow. The **perfect work** or result here is spiritual maturity— become **perfect**—as it is in Galatians 3:3 and Colossians 1:28. It is being spiritually grown up, and no longer a baby in the faith. (cf. 1 Corinthians 3:1; Hebrews 5:13) The term **entire** is the Greek ὁλόκληρος (holokleros), a compound

---

25 David R. Anderson, *Triumph Through Trials*, 10–11.

word that means "pertaining to being complete and meeting all expectations, *with integrity, whole, complete, undamaged, intact, blameless.*" The point is being **entire, wanting** or lacking **nothing** in terms of the full benefits intended for us as a result of the trial.

Pulling all of this together, we should intellectually **count it all joy** about the trials of life based on our understanding of the relationship between trials and our spiritual growth. When we meet the trials in reliance on God's provision and His Word, we demonstrate proven **faith**, and that quality of **faith** produces **patience** or steadfast endurance under His will for us as we work the pop quizzes and major exams successfully. The trials that produce steadfast endurance are part of God's training program to bring us to spiritual maturity. Everyone faces trials, big and small, but God especially uses trials to grow His children to maturity. And while we are not told to relish the trial itself, James says we can have **joy** in the trial knowing God is at work in and through us to bring us to maturity.

> **James 1:5** If any of you lack wisdom, let him ask of God, that giveth to all *men* liberally, and upbraideth not; and it shall be given him. **6** But let him ask in faith, nothing wavering. For he that wavereth is like a wave of the sea driven with the wind and tossed. **7** For let not that man think that he shall receive any thing of the Lord. **8** A double minded man *is* unstable in all his ways.

Having set out the critical relationship between faith, trials and spiritual growth, James turns to a specific provision of God to face the trials. Sometimes life presents us with trials for which there is a clear Biblical directive. For example, if an employer would require us to engage in unlawful or dishonest activities in the course of doing our jobs, the Bible contains clear directives that should guide our response to our employer. Our faith response will require us to refuse to engage in the unlawful or dishonest activity. But life's issues are not always so clear cut, and often we face decisions that do not directly implicate the clear moral directives in the Bible. Even where there is a clear moral directive in the Bible, we may still need **wisdom** to guide how we respond. It is not just knowing the truth of God's Word, but having skill in employing its principles.

Anticipating this, James says, **if any of you lack wisdom, let him ask of God, that giveth to all *men* liberally, and upbraideth not; and it shall be given him**. James' exhortation, in the face of the challenges, decisions and trials of life, is to pray to **God** for **wisdom**. There is a **faith** element in praying for **wisdom**. We should understand that **God...giveth to all men liberally** or generously and that **God...upbraideth not**. In other words, **God** gives **wisdom** generously without reprimanding us for asking. This is trusting in the provision of **God** for the moment that I alluded to earlier. Trusting in the provision of **God** for the trial we face prompts us to pray for God's **wisdom**. The opposite is self-reliance, which is rooted in pride. What may be just beneath the surface here becomes more apparent as the epistle unfolds. We need humility. But there is another aspect of the **faith** element, which is a willingness and readiness to follow the **wisdom** God provides. Many people relate to the experience of someone confiding in them about a trial they are facing and asking for advice. The advice is given and six weeks later a similar conversation occurs again, with the same person providing an update on their problem. The one who gave the advice asks whether they followed the advice. No, they did not, but now they want further advice. If that advice is given, the cycle will repeat again. People will do the same thing with God. Asking with no intent of following through on the **wisdom** is not asking in **faith**. Moreover, asking in prayer a few times then falling back on worldly **wisdom** is not asking in **faith**.

Consequently, there is a warning. James anticipates our need for **wisdom** but also the Christian with the half-hearted "going through the motions" type of prayer that is quickly followed with a return to self-reliance, or is prayed with no genuine expectation that God will do what He promised, or no genuine intent to receive God's **wisdom**. Thus, James exhorts the person in the trial to **ask** or pray **in faith, nothing wavering** or doubting about God's provision. This is a prayer that trusts God in His timing to provide the **wisdom** that is needed at the moment and with the intent of following God's **wisdom**. James continues, **for he that wavereth** or doubts (i.e. lacks **faith**) **is like a wave of the sea driven with the wind and tossed.** We must connect this back to the opening verses and the quality or character of **faith** that produces endurance—a **faith** that relies on God's resources and His Word. What James describes here is the opposite—a person that is not making faithful decisions by applying God's Word and **wisdom** to the circumstances of life. They are untethered, being **tossed** about in their thinking as they try to work out their problem on their own resources, unable to fix upon a solution. The doubting Christian should **not...think that he shall receive any thing of the Lord.** James characterizes the doubting Christian as **double minded**, meaning he or she is of two minds. This person is uncertain in their thinking and will not make a resolute decision to do life God's way. The result is that he or she **is unstable in all his** or her **ways.** This problem, ultimately a lack of **faith** in God's provision and Word, is not limited to the immediate trial they face. This characterizes their life. They lack the steadfast endurance that trials should bring and they lack the convictions of maturity. As long as they remain **double minded** they will never face trials well and never grow to maturity.

James returns in James 3:13-18 to the issue of **wisdom,** where he explains that there are two competing types of **wisdom**—one that emanates from the world and one from God. For our purposes at this point, note that "the wisdom that is from above is first pure, then peaceable, gentle, and easy to be intreated, full of mercy and good fruits, without partiality, and without hypocrisy." (James 3:17) Most of the challenges and trials we face require **wisdom** to come through the trial in such a way that our conduct honors God. We need the type of **wisdom** James describes in 3:17 to do that. Worldly **wisdom,** which James calls "earthly, sensual, devilish" (James 3:15), results in "confusion and every evil work" (James 3:16). Worldly **wisdom** is about selfish ambition. The last thing we need is worldly **wisdom** if we hope to exhibit proven faith in the face of trials.

Having said all of this, we should ask how God provides the **wisdom** He promises those who ask in **faith?** We should not expect that we just toss up a prayer for **wisdom** as we lay our head down to sleep and then mysteriously the next morning awaken with **wisdom.** A person who prays for God to provide them a job must couple the prayer with sending out resumes and putting their best foot forward in interviews. So also in this matter of **wisdom** there is something for us to do coupled with our prayer. Obviously, we need to listen to God's **wisdom** that is already in the Bible, and especially in places like the Proverbs. If we want to grow spiritually and learn God's **wisdom** we must have our heads in the Book. But also, we need to carefully research the decisions we are faced with. We need to have all the pertinent information. As Jesus said, "which of you, intending to build a tower, sitteth not down first, and counteth the cost, whether he have sufficient to finish it?" In addition, we need to recognize that God may minister **wisdom** to us from those around us. Much of the Proverbs are presented as Solomon talking to a son. Paul said in Titus 2:4 that the older women in the church should teach the younger women about family life, which means sharing wisdom with them. We need to establish friendships with mature Christians, generally older than us, that will provide mentoring and wisdom based on their experience.

> **James 1:9** Let the brother of low degree rejoice in that he is exalted: **10** But the rich, in that he is made low: because as the flower of the grass he shall pass away. **11** For the sun is no sooner risen with a burning heat, but it withereth the grass, and the flower thereof falleth, and the grace of the fashion of it perisheth: so also shall the rich man fade away in his ways. **12** Blessed *is* the man that endureth temptation: for when he is tried, he shall receive the crown of life, which the Lord hath promised to them that love him.

Sometimes readers fail to see how well organized James' epistle is and they view it as a hodge-podge of sayings or maxims. We need to see that in verses 9-12, James continues addressing the general subject matter of growing through trials that he has been addressing to this point. The trials of life do not discriminate. Wealthy people face trials just as poor people do. By implication, everyone in between faces trials. In his prologue, James provides perspective that believers need to have about trials and their relationship to faith and growth. The passage at hand provides further perspective on faith and trials. As trials do not discriminate, trials have a way of providing perspective for all believers regardless of their station in life.

James explains that the **brother** or Christian **of low degree** should **rejoice in that he is exalted**. James makes a contrast here between a Christian **of low degree** and one who is **rich**, and so James means by **low degree** one of humble financial means. We need to note that the Greek word translated **rejoice** is καυχάομαι (kochaomai) and has a primary meaning of "to take pride in something" and is typically translated as "*boast, glory, pride oneself, brag.*" James says, **let** the poor Christian boast or glory **in that he is exalted**. A natural question is how is the poor Christian **exalted**? That gets answered in verse 12 and we shall return to that question momentarily. But what we must observe is the contrasting perspectives of different believers. While the poor Christian may boast in his exaltation, James says **the rich** should boast **in that he is made low** or humbled. In both instances, the boasting has nothing to do with personal merit, but reflects a divine perspective on their circumstances.

James explains that **as the flower of the grass he**, meaning the rich Christian, **shall pass away**. James adds, **for the sun is no sooner risen with a burning heat, but it withereth the grass, and the flower thereof falleth, and the grace of the fashion of it perisheth; so also shall the rich man fade**

away in his ways. The world is passing away and so our perspective should not be wrapped up in things of the world like affluence and wealth. If the sum and substance of our lives is wrapped up in material things, our lives will **fade away** with those things and none of it will have eternal value. This speaks to what James perceived to be an obstacle for wealthy Christians, who are more prone to be self-reliant and not see the transitory nature of life and wealth. But trials will show this to the wealthy Christian, and this recognition and new perspective is reason to rejoice. Our Christian perspective should focus on things that last beyond the grave. But what really lasts? To that question, James offers what sounds like it could have come from the Beattitudes in Jesus' famous Sermon on the Mount.

Verse 12 explains why the poor Christian may boast in being **exalted** and the rich Christian in being **made low** by the tests and trials of life. He says, **blessed** or happy **is the man that endureth temptation**. The word translated as **temptation** is the Greek πειρασμός (peirasmos) that we saw in verse 2 ("count it all joy when ye fall into divers temptations") and has the same meaning here of the general tests and trials of life that come in all shapes and sizes. These statements in verses 2 and 12 form an inclusio, confirming that the subject throughout verses 2 to 12 is the same. The reason the Christian, rich or poor, that endures through the trials is **blessed** or happy is that **when he is tried, he shall receive the crown of life, which the Lord hath promised to them that love him**. We need to unpack a few of these words to properly interpret this blessing. Recall first that in verse 3 ("that the trying of your faith") the Greek word translated **trying** is the noun δοκίμιον (dokimion). The word translated **tried** in verse 12 is the related Greek adjective δόκιμος (dokimos). According to BDAG, it means "pertaining to being genuine on the basis of testing, *approved (by test), tried and true, genuine.*" As I noted about verse 3, it is not being tested that results in developing steadfast endurance under God's will, but passing the test, i.e., being approved or proven by handling the test or trial on the basis of faith in God's Word and His provision. The meaning is the same here, namely that a believer is **blessed when he** is approved or proven, that is, when his faith is shown to be proven faith that produces steadfast endurance. But what exactly is the additional blessing James has in mind?

James writes that as a result of being approved, **he shall receive the crown of life**. First, note the time-marker for when the **crown** is received. It is **when he is tried** or approved, meaning when the trial is successfully completed. While in other contexts there is reference to crowns received after this mortal life, that is not the case here. As Anderson writes: "This crown is usually explained as something a faithful believer receives after this life is over at the Judgment Seat of Christ. But if we look carefully, the text says we get this crown after we have endured the trial and come out without cracks—approved. That happens in this life."[26] The **crown** is not what we usually visualize—a metal crown or tiara worn by a king or queen. Rather, it is a στέφανος (stephanos), which is a wreath made of foliage awarded as a prize for winning a sports contest or as an award for some other achievement. Its use here is metaphorical, for there is no real, physical **crown** being provided. The metaphor emphasizes its nature as a reward for steadfast endurance through a trial.

---

[26] David R. Anderson, *Triumph Through Trials*, 36.

39

But what is **the crown of life**? This will become more apparent as we explore the next few verses since they provide a contrast to verse 12. As Hodges writes, "It seems much more likely, however, that James has in mind the way God enriches our *present* experience of life, when testing has been successfully endured."[27] The **crown of life** is the reward of experiencing the abundant or victorious **life** now that results from spiritual growth through trials that develop endurance. Linking together what James says, we all face challenges and trials, both rich and poor Christians and all those in between. God uses the challenges and trials of life to prove our faith in His provisions and His Word. Proven faith develops steadfast endurance, and when the trial is successfully endured on the basis of faith in God and His provision, the believer is rewarded with a greater experience of **life** (in the here and now). Note that James adds, **which the Lord hath promised to them that love him**. Those that **love him** obey his commands. (John 14:15, 21) To them that obey his commands, Jesus promised, "he that loveth me shall be loved of my Father, and I will love him, and will manifest myself to him." This suggests to us a greater experience of intimacy with the Saviour, and that is what James is getting at as well. As we will see below, there are those that lack love for God and instead blame Him for their sin; they receive no **crown of life**.

We tend to think of eternal **life** in terms of duration and future destiny, but eternal **life** is also now. We will not all experience eternal **life** in the same way now. Many Christians wrongly assume that their experience of the Christian **life** is the same as other Christians' experiences

---

[27] Zane C. Hodges, Arthur L. Farstad, and Robert N. Wilkin, *James*, 25.

and it may not be. Those who are spiritually growing, especially through trials (big and small), will experience **life** in a deeper and more profound way that we might call the abundant **life** (John 10:10: "I am come that they might have life, and that they might have it more abundantly") or reigning in **life** (Romans 5:17: "...much more they which receive abundance of grace and of the gift of righteousness shall reign in life by one, Jesus Christ"). Paul says to Timothy, "Fight the good fight of faith, lay hold on eternal life..." (1 Timothy 6:18) To lay hold on eternal **life** is to experience more **life** by drawing nearer to God through developing a more intimate relationship with Jesus Christ. Those whose faith is not proven, because they fail the tests by failing to respond to the trials of life with a Biblical perspective and on the basis of God's provisions and His Word, are not spiritually maturing and as a consequence are not experiencing **life** to the fullest degree available to them. As Anderson states:

> We need never be overwhelmed by any circumstance because we have an infinite Lord who is ready for anything and who amply equips us. When we have laid hold of our Lord we will discover He is adequate for anything. Through Him we are victors in battle and we can wear the crown of life. I really think this crown of life is true happiness. It isn't just a laugh or a smile. It's deep inner peace, that bubbling of living waters springing up within. It is the deep satisfaction of having finished a difficult task, of having finished the race.[28]

---

[28] David R. Anderson, *Triumph Through Trials*, 36.

There are serious consequences to not growing spiritually. That being the case, we can understand why James' epistle focuses on the conduct and thinking that will foster or frustrate our growth.

> **James 1:13** Let no man say when he is tempted, I am tempted of God: for God cannot be tempted with evil, neither tempteth he any man: **14** But every man is tempted, when he is drawn away of his own lust, and enticed. **15** Then when lust hath conceived, it bringeth forth sin: and sin, when it is finished, bringeth forth death.

In contrast to the Christian that faces trials with the proper perspective, seeing their faith proven and growth in their life as they learn steadfast endurance, some fail their tests (over and over). In the face of difficulties, they turn to sin and blame God. Perhaps they reason that God left them no choice or coerced them. James addresses this issue because it is real possibility for all of us, especially when we are under pressure. But he admonishes the believer that would respond in this way: **Let no man say when he is tempted, I am tempted of God.** The word **tempted** is the Greek verb πειράζω (peirazō) and is related to the noun πειρασμός (peirasmos) that we saw in verses 2 and 12, translated there as "temptation." As already noted, the word can have the idea of a temptation or enticement to sin or may simply refer to the general tests and trials of life. In verses 2 and 12, James used peirasmos to refer to trials. Here, James uses the word in the sense of being subjectively enticed to sin, which is a possibility in dealing with most any type of trial. That this is James' intent is made clear by the statement that **God cannot be tempted**

with evil, neither tempteth he any man. While God may bring the trial, He never entices people to sin their way out of the trial or sin in response to the trial. And while we know Satan may do that, James makes no mention of that here. He lays the issue 100% at our feet: **But every man is tempted** (again, peirazō), **when he is drawn away of** or by **his own lust, and enticed.** We should note that James likely has the experience of Job in mind (see James 5:11); God permitted Job's trials but never enticed him to sin.

The phrase **drawn away** translates the Greek verb ἐξέλκω (exelkō) and means "to drag away, with connotation of initial reluctance." But the point here is not a literal dragging away. This Christian is no victim of anyone else. James says **every man** without exception who is **tempted** to sin **is drawn away of his own lust.** The word **lust** is the noun ἐπιθυμία (epithumia) and means (BDAG) "a great desire for something, *desire, longing, craving.*" The culprit is us—our own internal **lust** patterns draw us away from what is right before God. By our own **lust** we are **enticed.** The word **enticed** is the verb δελεάζω (deleazō) and means "to lure by the use of bait." (BDAG) It has been rightly observed that if we could at the moment of decision know the full consequences of our choices, many opportunities to sin would be passed by. But sin is enticing, like bait to a fish. The issue is what is between our ears—in our thought life. James draws a vivid picture of our own internal **lust** patterns fixating on something so that we are further baited or **enticed.**

James continues the progression from temptation to enticement, explaining that **when lust** or desire **hath conceived, it bringeth forth sin.** When our desires become impregnated, that which grows in our thought-life eventually gives birth to **sin**. And while other people and even Satan can influence us, they cannot force our hand. We have PhD's in sin and manage to do it all on our own. We cannot blame God. Sin promises (the enticement) so much but in the end fails to deliver. James says that **sin, when it is finished, bringeth forth** or gives birth to **death**. Of course, when we think of birth we think of the result being life. But ironically that is not the case here. The chain of causation James shows us is temptation rooted in our own internal lusts (in our hearts or minds), which leads to enticement, and as we continue in our thought-life feeding the **lust** it becomes impregnated and gives birth to **sin**. Our creed always determines our conduct. We are what we think, and what we think will determine what we do. As **sin** is completed or **finished** it gives birth to consequences, and that is **death**.

But what is **death** in this context? The contrast James draws is between (1) those who face trials in such a way that they endure and are rewarded with the "crown of life" and (2) those who turn to sin and reap **death**. James is not talking of physical **death** per se, but of the opposite of the "crown of life." Rather than being rewarded with abundant or victorious life based on handling the challenges and trials of daily living, poor choices based on following one's **lust** instead of God's Word and wisdom result in experiencing **death**, the opposite of the abundant life. People who are not Christians can only experience **death**. But Christians have a choice. How we live matters. How we live will determine if we experience **life** in the fullest sense or **death**. The notion of **death** entails separation. We can be Christians, who positionally are "in Christ," yet in our experience we do not have sense of intimacy with God. We lack inner peace, face routine anxiety and despair. We do well to remember Paul's words to the Christians in Rome: "For the wages of sin is death; but the gift of God is eternal life through Jesus Christ our Lord." (Romans 6:23) Paul addresses believers in Romans 6 about growing in the faith. When a Christian engages in **sin** he or she experiences **death**. But when they pursue God they experience in real time eternal **life**. We must make this personal—am I experiencing **life** or **death**? How you are handling trials will be a key indicator of whether you are wearing a crown of life.

> **James 1:16** Do not err, my beloved brethren.
> **17** Every good gift and every perfect gift is from above, and cometh down from the Father of lights, with whom is no variableness, neither shadow of turning.
> **18** Of his own will begat he us with the word of truth, that we should be a kind of firstfruits of his creatures.

James continues to address the same subject matter of our perspective and response to trials and how that relates to growth and experiencing life or death. Verses 2 through 18 covers this ground and leads to the "wherefore" of verse 19. Understanding the big picture argument, flow and structure of the book will be critical to properly interpreting the often disputed verses in chapter 2 that, in turn, tend to color our view of the entire epistle.

To the hypothetical Christian of verse 13 that claimed he was tempted to sin by God and ultimately experienced death, James says, **do not err** in your thinking on this matter, **my beloved brethren**. James speaks to his fellow believers, focusing on a proper perspective. God does not entice us to sin nor does He desire that we experience death. Rather, **every good gift and every perfect gift is from above, and cometh down from the Father of lights, with whom is no variableness, neither shadow of turning.** The picture of **variableness** and **shadow of turning** is that of heavenly bodies (like stars) that reflect a variance of light. But in contrast, the **Father of lights**, the One who created the heavens, does not change. God provides **every good gift** and will never provide anything else. God provides gifts that meet our needs, especially in our trials.

The chief example of a **good gift** from **the** unchanging **Father** is that **of his own will begat he us with the word of truth.** I note here that the NET translation reads: "By his sovereign plan he gave us birth through the message of truth." But there is nothing in the Greek text that says "sovereign plan." It is a good lesson for us that translations may reflect theological biases and we do not have the right to force our theological commitments over the text. The NET notes concede as much, saying the Greek is literally, "Having willed, he gave us birth." In accordance with God's **will** or desire He **begat...us.** The **begat** is aorist or past tense action, and **us** refers to James and his audience collectively as Christians. The **gift** of God is that He brought them forth or gave them the new birth so that they became His children. But like all gifts, it must be received. This was accomplished **with the word** or message **of truth**, which refers to the gospel. James writes to fellow Christians and therefore does not need to remind them of the complete content of the **word of truth.** Eternal salvation is the ultimate **good gift** from the **Father of lights**, and we know from dozens of passages that it is received through faith.

Finally, James notes that God's **gift** has a purpose, **that we should be a kind of firstfruits of his creatures.** In the Old

Testament, the concept of **firstfruits** referred to a portion of an agricultural harvest. Literal "firstfruits" of an agriculture harvest provided a sample of the expected full harvest. Here, literal crops are not in view, but the imagery is that James and his audience, as early Jewish Christians, are a **firstfruits** of God's people who became children of God in response to the **word of truth**. We have the benefit of looking back on nearly 2,000 years of church history and seeing the harvest so far. And we know there is more harvest to come.

Closing

Perspective can be as important as answers. The prologue to James provides some of both. Christians should expect and even welcome trials with the joy of knowing God is doing a work in our lives. Everyone has trials, but not everyone has a divine perspective on their trials. We are in God's training program for the world to come, and many of the most important lessons are learned as we endure through trials. On this issue, President Ronald Reagan wrote in a personal letter: "It takes a lot of fire and heat to make a piece of steel." This means when the trials come, we need to pray for God's wisdom to make sound decisions in how we respond to the trials, but also to help us understand what He would teach us through those trials. As we continue through this epistle, it will become apparent that the point James is making is that we need to know and live out God's Word. Remember that you cannot do what you do not know, and so we should seek to know God's Word better than we know anything else. But God's Word is not fully comprehended just from reading it. God's training course has a lab component that we call life. That is the classroom where we learn to live by faith, meaning apply and live out the truths of God's Word we claim with our lips to believe. The rewards of faithfulness through trials are endurance, the crown of life, and maturity.

Application Points

Main Principle: God uses the diverse tests and trials of life to teach us endurance, prove the quality of our professed faith in His Word, and grow us to spiritual maturity.

-- We need to know God's wisdom and His Word to face the trials of life.

-- God does not tempt us to sin even in our trials.

-- Every blessing we have is from God.

Discussion Questions

1. What are some examples of relatively routine tests / trials that you face? (at home, at work, at school, at church)

2. What does endurance look like in practical terms?

3. What does a lack of endurance look like in practical terms?

4. How is a "perfect" or mature believer different from an immature believer?

5. What are some benefits of being spiritually mature?

6. What are some consequences of never growing to spiritual maturity?

7. Who can you go to for wisdom when you face a trial?

8. Are trials harder or easier for poor Christians, middle-class Christians, or rich Christians?

9. James 1:17 says God never changes. Why is that important for us to know?

Chapter 3

God's Word Can Save Your Soul-Life

James 1:19-27

When we hear the word "save" or "saved," we may tend to think immediately in terms of someone being "saved" from the penalty of sin or saved from hell. But there are several Biblical senses in which these words are used. In particular, the New Testament has a great deal to say about saving the saved. The person without Christ needs to be saved so that they will spend eternity with God. But for the saved person—the Christian—there is still a type of saving they need. In particular, they need to be saved from the power or influence of sin in their lives because of their sin nature. This is the saving that leads to Christians demonstrating righteousness in their lives. Theologians refer to this aspect of salvation as sanctification, a word that denotes being set apart for God's purposes. The book of James is about sanctification, with a special focus given to one aspect—saving the soul-life. That special focus is the relationship between our faithfulness to living out

God's Word and the future judgment of our works. This future judgment, as it relates to the Christian, is not to determine our destiny. That was settled the moment we trusted Christ for the forgiveness of sins—the moment we were saved from sin's penalty. Rather, this future judgment concerns the extent to which we are rewarded for our faithfulness to God's Word. We saw in the prologue (1:2-18) that it is proven faith that endures trials and leads to maturity. Proven faith also produces works that are rewarded in the coming judgment. Making God's Word real in our lives is serious business, for we shall shortly stand before Jesus and give an account.

Outline

I. GREETING (1:1)

II. GOD USES TESTS AND TRIALS TO GROW US TO MATURITY (1:1-18)

III. <u>**CENTRAL EXHORTATION:**</u> THE CHRISTIAN GROWING TO MATURITY IS QUICK TO HEAR, SLOW TO SPEAK AND SLOW TO ANGER (1:19-20)

IV. GOOD HEARERS HUMBLY EMBRACE GOD'S IMPLANTED WORD AND LIVE IT OUT TO THE SAVING OF THE SOUL-LIFE AT THE JUDGMENT (1:21-2:26)

   a. <u>**Key Principle About Being Swift to Hear**</u>: Putting aside sin and humbly embracing God's Word can save your soul-life (1:21)

   b. Knowing God's Word does is not the same as embracing and experiencing His Word (1:22-27)

i. The attitude toward God's Word of someone who does not embrace it and apply it to life (1:23-24)

ii. The attitude toward God's Word of someone who embraces it and applies the law of liberty to life (1:25)

iii. The empty religion and self-deception of the person who does not embrace God's Word is revealed by his or her uncontrolled speech (1:26)

iv. The authentic religion of the person who does embrace God's Word is revealed by his or her application of the law of liberty to life (1:27)

Scripture and Comments

James now begins the main body of his epistle (1:19-5:6). The main body has three main sections, and in this chapter we will cover his high level thematic statement (1:19-20) that summarizes the crux of his epistle and then a portion of the first main section (1:21-27). Getting hold of the structure of James is critical to rightly dividing it. Too many expositors fail to account for the structure of the epistle and its overarching themes. After setting out his thematic statement, James turns to the critical issue of saving the saved.

> **James 1:19** Wherefore, my beloved brethren, let every man be swift to hear, slow to speak, slow to wrath: **20** For the wrath of man worketh not the righteousness of God.

The prologue (vv. 2-18) relates faith, trials and spiritual growth. James now presents the central exhortation in the book, summarizing the skillset we need to develop so that we might grow through our trials. He begins with **wherefore**, which looks back to the prologue and informs the reader he will state a conclusion grounded in what came before. James speaks with a pastor's heart to **my beloved brethren** or fellow Christians, exhorting **every man** or person to **be swift to hear, slow to speak, slow to wrath**. While being a good listener is an admirable trait, James is saying much more than that when he writes **be swift to hear**. The specific content he has in mind is God's wisdom and His Word. We see that because James addresses God's wisdom in verses 5-8, the "word of truth" in the prior verse, in verse 21 he exhorts his readers to **receive...the engrafted word**, and in verse 22 he exhorts them to be **doers of the word**. As I suggested earlier, God's Word is part of the content of faith tested by trials. Because it is God's wisdom and His Word that we need to **be swift to hear**, the exhortation means much more than good listening. We need to comprehend and apply God's Word to successfully handle the challenges and trials of life. For this reason, James expounds in verse 21 on how he wants his audience (and by application, us) to **hear** God's Word.

Before turning to how we should **hear** God's Word, James also says to **be...slow to speak**. The Bible says a great deal about our speech, especially in the wisdom literature. James addresses speech in every chapter. The importance of speech to our Christian walk cannot be overstated. To summarize what will come later, James says being able to control our speech is a hallmark of spiritual maturity and warns against the potential for destruction our speech has. As Christians, we should care a great deal about managing our speech so as to edify others. Jesus said that "every idle word that men shall speak, they shall give account thereof in the day of judgment." (Matthew 12:36) We are especially susceptible to saying the wrong things when we are facing trials and adversity. And so, James adds in the important qualifier, **be...slow**. He does not say to stop talking, but to be **slow to** talk. We should not just say whatever pops into our head. What comes out of our mouths should be deliberate, measured, thoughtful, and edifying. The right words may help us weather a trial, heal a relationship, encourage others, or even lead someone to Christ, while the wrong words may cause destruction.

James next says to **be...slow to wrath**. Our kneejerk reaction when faced with adversity may be to get angry— at God or those around us. But getting angry will not help us grow through a trial and being angry is the opposite of steadfast endurance, which God intends to be one of the products of our growth through trials. The reason is that **the wrath of man worketh not the righteousness of God.** Our anger will never accomplish God's righteousness in our lives. If God is using the trials we face to instill endurance and grow us spiritually, then anger is contrary to that goal and reflects that we are not enduring but buckling under pressure.

> **James 1:21** Wherefore lay apart all filthiness and superfluity of naughtiness, and receive with meekness the engrafted word, which is able to save your souls.

James begins the first section (1:21-2:26) of the main body of his epistle, elaborating on the exhortation to be "swift to hear." James expresses the overarching principle he will build through the balance of this unit of thought (1:21-2:26).

I cannot overstate the practical importance of the doctrine James explains in this section to our Christian walks. The concept of the "salvation of the soul" is pervasive in the New Testament, although frequently addressed in different terms like the bema judgment, judgment seat of Christ, crowns, inheritance, and rewards.

To get our hands around the relationship between the God's Word and the saving of our **souls**, we first need to focus on some important terms: **receive, engrafted, save** and **souls**. One of the central reasons the book of James is widely misunderstood is because terms are assumed to mean something they do not mean, and there is confusion about the words **save** and **souls**. The word **receive** is the Greek δέχομαι (dechomai) and is not a casual receiving but more like a welcoming embrace. We see the word used in the sense of welcoming in Matthew 10:14 ("whosoever shall not **receive** you, nor hear your words, when ye depart of that house or city, shake off the dusty of your feet") and Acts 7:59 (Stephen prays, "Lord Jesus, **receive** my spirit"). And in a very similar usage to the verse at hand, we read in Acts 17:11 about the Bereans welcoming God's Word: "These were more noble than those in Thessalonica, in that they **received** the word with all readiness of mind, and searched the scriptures daily, whether those things were so." So when James says **receive with meekness** or humility **the engrafted word**, it is the idea of a welcoming embrace of God's **word** with an attitude of humility (not pride). The word **engrafted** is from a primary verb φύω (phuō) that Strong's defines as "to germinate or grow (sprout, produce), literally or figuratively:--spring (up)." And so the imagery James uses is humbly welcoming God's **word** into our hearts like soil embraces a seed so that it may germinate and spring up. Apart from this embracing, the **word** will not have its intended effect, which is our growth to maturity.

The word **save** is the Greek verb σώζω (sōzō) and means to deliver and context must determine from what someone is being saved or delivered. Because in a church context we tend to associate the words "save" and "saved" with being saved from the penalty of sin or being saved from hell, this meaning is often carelessly assumed when people read a verse like James 1:21 that uses the term **save**. But in fact, this Greek verb, and the related noun σωτηρία (soteria), more often than not do not concern being delivered from the penalty of sin or hell. The verb **save** is used 109 times in the New Testament, and as J.B. Hixson shows, more than 60% of those uses are not in the context of being saved from the penalty of sin.[29] Some examples will illustrate:

- Delivered from the penalty of sin (Acts 16:30-31: "And brought them out, and said, Sirs, what must I do to be saved? And they said, Believe on the Lord Jesus Christ, and thou shalt be saved, and thy house.") (sōzō)

- Delivered from illness (Mark 5:25-34: "thy faith hath made thee whole") (sōzō)

- Delivered from sleep (John 11:12: "if he [Lazarus] sleep, he shall do well [wake up]") (sōzō)

- Delivered from temporal judgment (Acts 2:40: "save yourselves from this untoward generation [of Israel]") (sōzō)

- Deliverance from Egypt (Acts 7:25: "that God by his hand would deliver them") (soteria)

---

[29] J. B. Hixson, *Getting the Gospel Wrong: The Evangelical Crisis No One Is Talking About*, Revised Edition. (Duluth, MN: Grace Gospel Press, 2013), 69–70.

- Delivered from drowning (Acts 27:20, 31: "except these abide in the ship, ye cannot be saved") (sōzō)

- Delivered from prison (Philippians 1:19: "this shall turn to my salvation through your prayer") (soteria)

James tells us that if we humbly welcome the **engrafted word**, it **is able to save** our **souls**. Like the word **save**, and like most words, the Greek word ψυχή (psuchē) carries different meanings in different contexts but is not the same as the word "spirit" (pneuma) as many assume. David Anderson explains that there are four New Testament uses of "soul" but it rarely refers to the immaterial aspect of man that can go to heaven or hell:

> The word *psychē* is used in four primary ways in the NT. Only a handful of the 104 uses refer to the immaterial part of man, which enjoys heaven or suffers in hell. Most of the time, the word refers either to our time on earth (our life) or to our inner self as a unique combination of mind (with one *psychē* striving together—Phil. 2:17), emotions (Mk 14:34—my *psychē* is exceedingly sorrowful), and will (doing the will of God from the *psychē*).[30]

We frequently see *psychē* translated as "soul" or "life" in our New Testaments. One use of **soul** is for the principle of life or being alive, as in Acts 20:10 (Eutychus fell out of the window and apparently died but "Paul went down, and fell on him, and embracing him said, Trouble not yourselves; for his **life** is in him."). Another use is for a

---

living human being, as in 1 Corinthians 15:44 ("The first man Adam was made a living soul...."). Yet another use is to refer to the entire immaterial aspect of man, as in Matthew 10:28 ("And fear not them which kill the body, but are not able to kill the **soul**: but rather fear him which is able to destroy both **soul** and body in hell."). And the fourth use is the experience of life, which may refer to experiences within the inner self as Anderson notes, or to the entire experience. Harry Leafe rightly explains that in the context of James 1:21, *psuchē* "describes the whole of a person's life" and "can be defined as *the total temporal expression of human life.*"[31] And again taking a cue from Leafe, we might express this concept as the "soul-life."

With this in mind, we can begin to understand in what sense humbly welcoming God's **word** can result in saving or delivering our soul-lives. Understanding the structure of James' epistle is also critical. His focus throughout 1:21-2:26 will be on living out God's **word** and how that relates to a future judgment of our works. James first explains further about what it means to humbly welcome God's word and he illustrates by focusing on the "royal law" or the "law of liberty," which is loving God and loving others. (James 1:22-27) James then demonstrates how the "royal law" or "law of liberty" relates to a local church context where favoritism or partiality might be shown to wealthy people over poor people. (James 2:1-7) He then relates how we live out the "royal law" / "law of liberty" to the coming judgment where our soul-lives will be measured against the standard of the "royal law" / "law of liberty." (James 2:8-13) In fact, James says that we should live "as they that shall be judged by the law of liberty." (James 2:12)

---

[31] G. Harry Leafe, *Running to Win!*, 4-5.

Several New Testament passages reference a future judgment on our soul-lives. Jesus explicitly teaches this concept to his disciples, warning them that those who will save their soul-life (i.e., live for themselves) will lose it at this future judgment, but those that lose their soul-life (i.e., live for Jesus) will save their soul-life at the future judgment. (e.g., Matthew 16:24-28; Luke 9:23-27) It is critical to observe that in these verses *it is the person who does the saving of their own soul-life*, which eliminates the possibility that justification, which is by grace, is in view. For a person to save their soul-life is for them to live so as to be rewarded by Jesus at the future judgment. (Matthew 16:27) As Anderson explains of Matthew 16: "That the passage in Matthew is not a Go-To-Heaven passage is clear from verse 27, which says Jesus will come back someday and 'reward' each man according to his deeds. It is about rewards, not getting to heaven."[32] A notable example we previously touched upon in the notes on James 1:3 is 1 Peter 1:3-9. What James says mirrors what Peter says. The entire book of 1 Peter concerns the salvation of the **soul**. Peter relates receiving an inheritance reserved in heaven for believers (1 Peter 1:4), which he calls a "salvation ready to be revealed in the last time" (1:5), to a present experience of trials (1:6-7). Peter says that their proven faith through those trials is "much more precious than gold" and will "be found unto [their] praise and honour and glory at the appearing of Jesus Christ." (1 Peter 1:7) Peter speaks of this future appraisal of their faith and the commendation from Jesus Christ as "receiving the end of your faith, even the salvation of your souls." (1 Peter 1:9)

---

[32] David R. Anderson, *Triumph Through Trials*, 60.

In God's progressive revelation, the apostle Paul writes that "we must all appear before the judgment seat of Christ; that every one may receive the things *done* in *his* body, according to that he hath done, whether *it be* good or bad." (2 Corinthians 5:10) Also in Romans 14:10, Paul says of believers, "for we shall all stand before the judgment seat of Christ." The "judgment seat" of Christ is the Greek *bema* and so many refer to this judgment as the "bema judgment." A *bema* was a special seat where a governing authority would sit and render decisions. Paul provides significant details of the bema judgment in 1 Corinthians 3:10-15, explaining that our works broadly fall into two baskets: (1) "gold, silver, precious stones" and (2) "wood, hay, stubble." (1 Corinthians 3:12) Using this imagery, our works will be tried by fire, and what survives the fire (i.e., the gold, silver, precious stones) will be rewarded. (1 Corinthians 3:14-15) It is in that sense—exchanging the product of our lives (i.e., our soul-lives) for rewards—that we can save our soul-life as Jesus teaches in Matthew 16. The issue is not whether we are destined for heaven or hell because that was dealt with at the cross and we were "saved" from sin's penalty the moment we trusted Christ. Rather, the issue is the quality of our faithfulness to God's Word as shown by our works. A natural question is what part of our soul-lives will be judged at the bema. The answer broadly speaking is our thoughts (1 Corinthians 4:3-5), words (Matthew 12:36), and actions (2 Corinthians 5:10). In particular, when we live out the royal law, that part of our soul-life (our experience of life) is what Paul refers to as "gold, silver, precious stones" that will be rewarded. When we live out our selfish and self-serving heart motivations, or live in a way that is rich toward the world and not rich toward God, that is what

Paul refers to as "wood, hay, straw," which will only earn smoke and ashes at the judgment. Paul imagines a hypothetical Christian at the bema whose entire soul-life goes up in smoke with no "gold, silver, precious stones." We might ask what that person's life looked like, but we cannot question their destiny, for Paul says "he himself shall be saved; yet so as by fire." (1 Corinthians 3:15) Other places in the New Testament put more color on what the rewards are. (e.g., 1 Peter 1:7; Luke 19:17-19)

Turning back to our text, James says to **lay apart all filthiness** (or moral filth) **and superfluity of naughtiness** (evil). He then says to humbly **receive** or welcome **the engrafted word, which is able to save your souls.** As we shall find as we continue through the end of James 2, the critical principle is that if we welcome God's **word** as soil embraces a seed for growth such that it becomes lived out truth, that expression of our **soul-life** will be saved or delivered at the (bema) judgment of our works. Anderson states it well: "If I were to ask you what you are going to do with your life, you would know that by 'life' I mean the rest of your time on earth. Once we are born again, the countdown begins. The issue becomes whether we will 'save' our time on earth (our lives) for our own selfish purposes or if we will dedicate our time on earth (our lives) to seeking first the kingdom of God."[33] This future judgment is not about heaven or hell. It is about Jesus assessing the quality of our faith and rewarding us for that part of our soul-lives that constitutes gold, silver, and precious stone. That is what **save your souls** is all about— faithfulness to God's **word** in our daily lives results in a soul-life that will be exchanged for eternal rewards at the

---

[33] David R. Anderson, *Triumph Through Trials*, 60.

bema judgment. That being the case, we need to learn our Bibles like our soul-lives depend on it because we cannot do (live out) what we do not know.

> **James 1:22** But be ye doers of the word, and not hearers only, deceiving your own selves. **23** For if any be a hearer of the word, and not a doer, he is like unto a man beholding his natural face in a glass: **24** For he beholdeth himself, and goeth his way, and straightway forgetteth what manner of man he was. **25** But whoso looketh into the perfect law of liberty, and continueth *therein*, he being not a forgetful hearer, but a doer of the work, this man shall be blessed in his deed.

James expounds on what it means to humbly welcome God's **word**. He has a tremendous warning for his audience and for us. The *single biggest lie Christians believe* is that "I know the truth therefore I experience it." Thus the warning, **be ye doers of** God's **word, and not hearers only.** We need to focus on the next clause— **deceiving your own selves**. There are many people that know a good amount of the Bible and assume they have a level of spiritual maturity and are experiencing God's truth in their lives. But many are self-deceived because knowing the truth does not automatically translate into experiencing the truth.

To aid our understanding of this landmine to our spiritual growth, James illustrates with a person that knows the truth but fails to humbly embrace it as the implanted **word,** and another person that both knows the truth and humbly embraces it. In both cases, James uses the metaphor of someone standing before a mirror and observing themselves in light of God's **perfect law of liberty.** It is their response to what they see that makes the difference.

In the first illustration, James presents a hypothetical person that is **a hearer of the word, and not a doer.** This person knows the truth, but fails to live it out. He is likened **unto a man beholding his natural face in a glass** or mirror. As the CSB notes indicate, the Greek translated **natural face** is literally "the face of his birth." The NET notes similarly indicate that the Greek is "the face of his beginning." For this reason, some understand James to be saying that this person **beholdeth himself** in the mirror and sees the **face** of his new birth in Jesus Christ. Essentially, he sees all that he should become as he expresses God's Word in his daily living. Most expositors understand this person to be seeing himself (**natural face**) in the mirror, with flaws made evident by his hearing **of the word.** In either understanding, the gist of the illustration remains the same. This hypothetical person does not keep his focus on what he sees in the mirror and the implications of God's Word for his life, and instead **goeth his way, and straightway forgetting what manner of man he was** in the mirror. This hypothetical person looked at himself through the lens of God's **word** for a moment, hearing the truth, but shortly after left the mirror—stopped thinking on God's **word** and forgot about its implications. We can imagine someone hearing a wonderful sermon on Sunday morning and seeing how they should change their life in light of God's **word,** but then forgetting it on Monday at work. It is not so much that they could not recall the sermon if asked, but they forget in the sense that they do nothing with what they learned and simply go about their business unchanged by

God's **word**. This person fails to humbly embrace God's **word** and as a result it will not save their soul-life. Truth that is not lived out is not rewarded at the judgment no matter how well you know it.

The second person **looketh into the perfect law of liberty, and continueth therein, he being not a forgetful hearer, but a doer of the work**. This person looks into the mirror of God's **word** to see himself living in light of God's truth, and specifically in James' illustration, living the **law of liberty**. James refers to the **law of liberty** in 1:25 and 2:12, and to the "royal law" in 2:8, and in each instance apparently refers to, "Thou shalt love thy neighbour as thyself." (James 2:8) James more broadly has in mind Jesus' teaching to love God and love others and so fulfill the righteousness of the Law and the prophets. (Matthew 22:37-40) Although James' principle in 1:21 is to embrace the "engrafted word" in general, his application through the end of chapter 2 will be on the royal law specifically. This makes sense because every sin in one way or another violates the royal law, and James is aware of specific failures to love others, as we will see.

This hypothetical person that looks into the mirror and sees how God's **perfect law of liberty** speaks to and will transform his life, and instead of leaving and forgetting the changes that need to be made, he **continueth therein**. He never leaves the mirror because he humbly embraces God's implanted **word**. The truth becomes lived truth as he is a **doer of the work**, and that is the only kind of truth that results in the saving of the soul-life at the judgment. That is why James adds, in reference to the coming judgment, **this man shall be blessed in his deed**, meaning **blessed in** what he does.

> **James 1:26** If any man among you seem to be religious, and bridleth not his tongue, but deceiveth his own heart, this man's religion *is* vain. **27** Pure religion and undefiled before God and the Father is this, To visit the fatherless and widows in their affliction, *and* to keep himself unspotted from the world.

The big delusion is assuming that knowing the truth means experiencing it. James returns in 1:26 to the self-deception of 1:22. In James' mind, there is self-deceived **religion** where a **man among you** (in your church) **seem to be** or thinks he is **religious**. However, he **bridleth not his tongue**, meaning he does not control his speech. Recall we noted earlier that at the judgment our thoughts, words, and actions will be assessed. Our speech matters, and indeed James' thematic statement in 1:19 was to "be swift to hear, slow to speak, slow to wrath." James addresses speech in all five chapters of his epistle. The inability to control our speech is a hallmark of spiritual immaturity. This person believes he is **religious**, suggesting some level spiritual maturity, but his speech betrays the reality that he **deceiveth his own heart**. His **religion is vain** or futile or useless. But how is it **vain** / useless? It bears repeating that James is not talking about eternal destiny. Many Christians who think highly of themselves will leave the bema judgment with nothing but smoke and ashes. (James 2:12-13) They are **religious** but not in the right way that saves the soul-life. They profess to believe Christians should love God and others, but they fail to consistently do it and may not realize it. James will expound on this kind of **religion** in chapter 2.

In contrast to such **vain** religion that fails to love God and others, **pure religion and undefiled before God and the Father is this, To visit the fatherless and widows in their affliction, and to keep himself unspotted** or unstained **from the world.** Remember what James says: "lay apart all filthiness and superfluity of naughtiness, and receive with meekness the engrafted word." If we focus on the **perfect law of liberty** or "royal law" as James does—love God and love others—this description presents someone whose life expresses the royal law. This person's **religion** is not just what he or she knows, but is lived truth. This person not only knows and professes to believe the royal law, but actually carries it out by caring for orphans and **widows.** The command to love God entails putting the things of God first and turning from worldliness, and this person does that, staying unstained **from the world.** This is a practical picture of a person that humbly welcomes the implanted word and lives it out. That is the **pure religion** that is not **vain** or useless at the coming bema judgment because it will be rewarded.

Closing

The purity of gold is measured in karats. Pure gold that is not alloyed with other metals is referred to as 24k gold. We may purchase gold that is 18k for example, and that means it is 75% gold and 25% alloyed metals. Similarly, 14k gold is 58% gold and 42% alloyed metals. We can even purchase 10k gold, which is less than 50% gold. Gold jewelry is usually not available in less than 10k, but suppose for illustration sake that a husband who has the financial wherewithal to buy his wife a 14k or 18k ring instead presents her with a 2k gold ring he bought on sale.

That would mean it is 8.3% gold and the rest relatively worthless metals. If you viewed faith like gold, what karat would your faith be? Would you say you love the Lord with 18k faith? What would 2k faith look like? I think many Christians' faith is not where they think it is. They are the hearers James warns about who know something of God's Word but fail to carry it out in their daily lives. In particular, they never change. They leave the mirror of the Word and forget what they saw. As James will show in James 2, we will all stand before Jesus and the quality of our faith will be examined. Will we show up with 2k faith—a life almost exclusively characterized by living for ourselves rather than living out God's Word?

Application Points

Main Principle: Christians need to set aside immorality and humbly welcome God's implanted Word such that they become doers of the Word, knowing it is able to save their soul-lives at the coming (bema) judgment.

-- The biggest lie Christians believe is that "I know the truth, therefore I experience the truth" in my daily life.

Discussion Questions

1. What is the relationship between humility (meekness) and being transformed by God's Word?

2. In practical terms how do we lay apart immorality as James says in 1:21?

3. How might we deceive ourselves into believing we are mature when we are not doers of the word?

4. Why is it that knowledge of God's Word does not always translate into action (good works)?

5. How might our speech demonstrate we lack spiritual maturity?

6. Why do you think James uses the care of widows and orphans to demonstrate what "pure religion" looks like?

7. What are some practical examples of how you can live out the royal law by providing for the needs of those most vulnerable in your society?

Chapter 4

The Coming Judgment
for Believers

James 2:1-26

Several years ago I polled a large Sunday school class in a theologically conservative Baptist church to see who had any understanding of the doctrine of rewards at the bema judgment. Most of these people had been in church for over a decade as adults and none had any idea about this doctrine. I do not think this is an isolated problem. This doctrine may be the most important ignored doctrine in the New Testament. The doctrine of rewards at the bema judgment is not an obscure matter hidden in the corner of our Bibles, but is pervasive in the New Testament. If God teaches something once in the Bible, it is important to learn it because it is part of God's Word and is "profitable for doctrine, for reproof, for correction, for instruction in righteousness." (2 Timothy 3:16) But if something is repeatedly taught in the Bible, such as salvation through faith alone and not works, then we should accept that as critical information insofar as God saw fit in His inspiration of Scripture to repeat and build out that truth. The doctrine of rewards is sometimes taught in the Bible using different words like account, rest, rewards, treasure, and inheritance. Not everything the Bible has to say about this matter is contained in James. In God's progressive revelation, the doctrine of rewards is introduced in Jesus' teaching in the Gospels and built out in the New Testament epistles. The material before us in James 2 is important to understanding the relationship between our faithfulness to living out God's Word and the coming judgment of our works.

Outline

I. GREETING (1:1)

II. GOD USES TESTS AND TRIALS TO GROW US TO MATURITY (1:1-18)

III. **CENTRAL EXHORTATION:** THE CHRISTIAN GROWING TO MATURITY IS QUICK TO HEAR, SLOW TO SPEAK AND SLOW TO ANGER (1:19-20)

IV. GOOD HEARERS HUMBLY EMBRACE GOD'S IMPLANTED WORD AND LIVE IT OUT TO THE SAVING OF THE SOUL-LIFE AT THE JUDGMENT (1:21-2:26)

    a. **Key Principle About Being Swift to Hear**: Putting aside sin and humbly embracing God's Word can save your soul-life (1:21)

    b. Knowing God's Word does is not the same as embracing and experiencing His Word (1:22-27)

c. Our obedience to the law of liberty (royal law) will be approved at the judgment and save our soul-life (2:1-26)

    i. A practical example – showing favoritism in the church based on wealth violates the law of liberty (royal law) (2:1-7)

        1. Favoring the wealthy reveals sinful motives (2:1-4)

        2. Favoring the wealthy ignores that it is the poor in the world that will inherit in the kingdom (2:5-7)

    ii. Fulfilling the royal law will find approval at the judgment (2:8-13)

        1. The royal law is to love others (2:8)

        2. Favoritism violates the royal law and makes one a transgressor (2:9-11)

        3. The law of liberty is the standard applied at the judgment to our speech and actions (2:12-13)

    iii. Knowing and believing God's Word without also living it out will not profit us at the judgment (2:14-26)

        1. The first faith-works inclusio: a faith without works will not save your soul-life at the judgment (2:14-17)

        2. The diatribe against the hypothetical objector (2:18-19)

        3. The second faith-works inclusio: a faith without works is useless (2:20-26)

Scripture and Comments

In the prior chapter we covered James' thematic statement in 1:19-20 and a portion (1:21-27) of the first section in the main body of his epistle (1:21-2:26). As we move forward, keeping the structure of the epistle in mind is critical. Too many expositors botch James 2:14-26 because they do not place it within and relate it to the entire unit that started in 1:21.

> **James 2:1** My brethren, have not the faith of our Lord Jesus Christ, *the Lord* of glory, with respect of persons. **2** For if there come unto your assembly a man with a gold ring, in goodly apparel, and there come in also a poor man in vile raiment; **3** And ye have respect to him that weareth the gay clothing, and say unto him, Sit thou here in a good place; and say to the poor, Stand thou there, or sit here under my footstool: **4** Are ye not then partial in yourselves, and are become judges of evil thoughts? **5** Hearken, my beloved brethren, Hath not God chosen the poor of this world rich in faith, and heirs of the kingdom which he hath promised to them that love him? **6** But ye have despised the poor. Do not rich men oppress you, and draw you before the judgment seats? **7** Do not they blaspheme that worthy name by the which ye are called?

James starts the first section of the main body of his epistle (James 1:21-2:26) with the charge to his readers to "lay apart all filthiness and superfluity of naughtiness, and receive with meekness the engrafted word, which is able to save your souls" (James 1:21). He then illustrates the difference between those that humbly welcome God's implanted Word and display in their lives their "pure religion," and those that do not and deceive themselves with "religion [that] is vain." (James 1:22-27) We have a tendency to hear good truth and quickly think of the people we know that need to hear that sermon. We can hear the "law of liberty" / "royal law" and quickly conclude that we live that truth. So James wants to stir the pot and step on some toes (good preachers do that). While James is teaching that we should humbly welcome all of God's implanted Word, He presses a practical illustration of how some people are self-deceived about their living out the easily understood "law of liberty" or "royal law" that we love others.

James introduces this subsection with **my brethren.** He refers to his audience 19 times as **brethren**, never questioning whether they are genuine believers. The exhortation is **not to** have **the faith of our Lord Jesus Christ, the Lord of glory, with respect of persons.** As we hold on to our **faith** in the **Lord Jesus Christ**, we should not show partiality among our brothers and sisters. We are repeatedly told in the Bible that God is no respecter of persons. (Acts 10:34; Romans 2:11; Ephesians 6:9; Colossians 3:25) In fact, **Jesus** never showed such partiality or favoritism. He was ridiculed because he ate with publicans and sinners. (Matthew 9:10-13) The "law of liberty" / "royal law" is violated if we hold our **faith...with respect of persons.**

James illustrates how this can happen. Suppose **there come unto your** church **assembly a man with a gold ring, in goodly apparel** (nice clothes), **and there come in also a poor man in vile raiment** (filthy clothes). By appearances, the first visitor has money and the second one does not. James continues the illustration, supposing that **ye have respect to him that weareth the gay** or fine **clothing,** telling him, **Sit thou here in a good place.** In contrast, the **poor** person is told, **Stand thou there, or sit here under my footstool.** We may have trouble relating to this example, but it is as appropriate today as ever. In some countries, Christian churches are divided by social class. There are churches for wealthy believers and churches for poor believers, and the two do not mix. The grandmother of a friend of mine attended a church in the United States that posted the giving of every member on the wall and assigned seating on that basis. The biggest givers took the first row, and those that gave the least sat at the back. The fact is that we often make judgments when we see people, and if we fail to live out the law of liberty we might treat people differently based on our subjective judgments. This has no place in a church, whether based on ethnicity or socio-economic class.

So James asks, **are ye not then partial in** or among **yourselves** in your church, **and are become judges** with **evil** motives? The answer to James' rhetorical question is yes, such partiality betrays wicked, unloving heart motivations. Favoring the **rich** over the **poor** spawns from covetous materialism, which is one of the primary sins plaguing churches in the United States at the present time. Such favoritism makes no sense. James admonishes them for this behavior, but again addressing them with a pastor's heart, as **my beloved brethren.** He asks, **Hath not God chosen the poor of this world rich in faith, and heirs of the kingdom which he hath promised to them that love him?** His point is that God saved many who are **poor in the world** in terms of money and possessions because they are

rich in faith. And while they are **poor** in **this world**, they are **heirs of the kingdom**, which is the true and lasting riches. It is absurd that James' audience has **despised the poor** that God has made **heirs of the kingdom**. Not only that, they show partiality to those that are wealthy even though **rich men oppress you, and draw you before the judgment seats**. They personally suffer oppression from wealthy people that carry influence in the courts, but then gush over the wealthy person that visits at church. Many of these wealthy oppressors **blaspheme that worthy** or noble **name by the which ye are called**. James' readers belong to Jesus, but some of the wealthy that they so admire **blaspheme** Jesus. That being the case, there is no basis for their being enamored with wealthy people. Christians today still gush over the rich and affluent.

James' point is that they show prejudice against a poor visitor at church who God says is an **heir of the kingdom**, while showing favoritism to rich visitors that come from the same group that oppress them and blaspheme Jesus. This is a flagrant violation of the royal law that they love others. How easy it is to look in the mirror then walk away and quickly forget. Everyone would agree we are to love others, and the command is easily understood, but we often fail to carry it out and are oblivious to it. Next, James will relate how we live out the truth of the "law of liberty" / "royal law" to the coming judgment.

> **James 2:8** If ye fulfil the royal law according to the scripture, Thou shalt love thy neighbour as thyself, ye do well: **9** But if ye have respect to persons, ye commit sin, and are convinced of the law as transgressors. **10** For whosoever shall keep the whole law,

and yet offend in one *point*, he is guilty of all. 11 For he that said, Do not commit adultery, said also, Do not kill. Now if thou commit no adultery, yet if thou kill, thou art become a transgressor of the law.

James explicitly states what he assumes his audience already knows, that the **royal law** is **Thou shalt love they neighbor as thyself.** He says it is **the royal law according to the scripture.** James' epistle is one of the earliest New Testament writings and for his Jewish Christian audience the **scripture** was the Old Testament. The Old Testament background for the royal law is Leviticus 19:18: "Thou shalt not avenge, nor bear any grudge against the children of thy people, but thou shalt love thy neighbour as thyself: I *am* the LORD." But of course, James and the early Christians knew that Jesus taught that this principle fulfilled the righteousness of the Old Testament Law and prophets:

> **Matthew 22:36** Master, which *is* the great commandment in the law? 37 Jesus said unto him, Thou shalt love the Lord thy God with all thy heart, and with all thy soul, and with all thy mind. 38 This is the first and great commandment. 39 And the second *is* like unto it, Thou shalt love thy neighbour as thyself. 40 On these two commandments hang all the law and the prophets.

As Harry Leafe comments, "These two commandments comprise what James variously calls 'The Perfect law' (1:25); 'The Law of Liberty' (1:25); and 'The Royal Law' (2:8). They touch every aspect and moment of life and teach us that our lives should be lived as those who will be judged by them (2:12)."[34] James says that **if ye fulfil the royal law... ye do well**. It may be, as many hold, that James uses the term **royal law** because this commandment was given by the king (Jesus). I think it more likely, as Lenski concludes, that the point is that the **royal law** is preeminent over all the commands of Jesus Christ:

> It is "royal," kingly, not because it emanates from God or from Christ as King; not because it applies to kings, or because it makes kings of those who obey it. It is "royal law" because it is sovereign over all other laws, is a law of such a quality that on it "hang all the law (Torah, Instruction) and the prophets" (the whole Old Testament, Matt. 22:40). "The whole law is fulfilled in one word, even in this: 'Thou shalt love thy neighbor as thyself.' " Gal. 5:14. Cf., 1 John 4:20.[35]

The reason **we do well** is because the **royal law** encapsulates the righteousness of "all the law and the prophets." But James also calls the **royal law** the law of liberty or freedom. (James 2:12) His point is not that his readers are obliged to keep the Old Testament Law. They are not going to be judged against the Mosaic Law, but will be judged by the law of liberty / **royal law**. (James 2:12-13). Every violation of God's holiness violates the **royal law** because in one way or another it fails to love God and others.

---

[34] G. Harry Leafe, *Running to Win!*, 22.

[35] R. C. H. Lenski, *The Interpretation of the Epistle to the Hebrews and of the Epistle of James* (Columbus, OH: Lutheran Book Concern, 1938), 570.

On the other hand, **if ye have respect to persons, ye commit sin**. This refers back to 2:1-7 and his illustration of showing partiality in a local church setting between a rich person and a poor person. The problem with being a "hearer of the word, and not a doer" (James 1:23) is that we are self-deceived. We fail to connect the dots in our lives between what we profess to believe and what we do. We leave the mirror of God's Word and forget, and so do not see ourselves as sinners when we fail to live out the truth. But James says those that show prejudice **are convinced** or convicted **of the law as transgressors** or violators. James' Jewish Christians, who previously lived under the Law until Jesus Christ inaugurated the New Covenant (e.g., Matthew 26:28; 1 Corinthians 11:25), would have continued to regard the Mosaic Law as encompassing the holiness of God in its moral precepts. His audience needs to understand that this is serious business because **whosoever shall keep the whole law, and yet offend in one point, he is guilty of all**. David Anderson provides helpful commentary on this issue:

> Here James turns to the law, both of Christ and of Moses. His point is simple. In effect, when you set the rich man ahead of the poor man, you are not loving that poor man. You are not treating him as you treat yourself. You would not like to be treated that way. Therefore you violate the royal law of love, and in so doing, all of the other morality you may claim is set aside. The law is a unit, a seamless garment. Break one link and you have broken the whole chain. Break part of a window and the whole window is shattered. If I go out and rob my

neighbor, it matters very little that I pay my taxes. I have constituted myself a criminal, a lawbreaker.[36]

The **royal law** in Leviticus 19:18 is part of the Old Testament Law of Moses, but it is also the **royal law** established by Jesus for his followers. To break just one law of Christ (like the **royal law**) makes you a law-breaker (**transgressor**), an indictment that would reverberate with his readers. James drives his point home with an illustration from the Ten Commandments that his audience would understand. Again, his point is not that they remain under the Mosaic Law as a covenant. His point is that just as breaking one of the laws of Moses under the old system made you a **transgressor** of all of it, so also breaking the **royal law** of Jesus Christ makes you a **transgressor** of the commands of Christ. James explains, **For he that said, Do not commit adultery, said also, Do not kill.** If you violate the latter (**if thou kill**) but do not do the former (**do not commit adultery**), you are still **a transgressor of the** entire **law** and that has consequences. As a **transgressor** of the **royal law** they should also expect to answer for their actions. This provides a segue to the coming judgment on their works. As James transitions to the issue of judgment, we need to recall the antecedent for this judgment in 1:21 where James says his readers should humbly receive the implanted Word because it is able to save their soul-lives.

> **James 2:12** So speak ye, and so do, as they that shall be judged by the law of liberty. **13** For he shall have judgment without mercy, that hath shewed no mercy; and mercy rejoiceth against judgment.

---

[36] David R. Anderson, *Triumph Through Trials*, 80–81.

James now explicitly answers the question raised by his exhortation in 1:21 that we should "receive with meekness the engrafted word, which is able to save your souls." The question raised was "save your souls" from what? And the answer, as suggested in the notes on 1:21, is that when we embrace God's Word it is able to save our soul-lives at the (bema) **judgment** as Christian works are rewarded. Again, James writes to believers, and so he necessarily has in mind a **judgment** for believers. This is not a **judgment** to determine our eternal destiny. That was settled at the moment they (and we) placed faith in Christ. Rather, this **judgment** concerns our works. James exhorts his readers (and us) to **so speak...and so do as they that shall be judged by the law of liberty.** As we have already seen, the **law of liberty** is another description of the royal law, namely the commandment to love God and others. Partiality in a local church setting is one way this **law** is violated.

Our thoughts, words and actions will **be judged** against the standard of **the law of liberty.** Recall from the notes on 1:21 that the issue at the bema **judgment** is works. James is so concerned about the issue of Christian speech that he addresses it in his thematic verse (see 1:19, "Wherefore, my beloved brethren, let every man be... slow to speak") and devotes substantial attention to it beginning in 3:1. James addresses Christian works in detail earlier in chapter 2 and picks up the issue again in 2:14. He also addresses our thought lives (our lusts) behind what we do and say. (e.g., James 1:14-15, 24; 3:14-16; 4:1-3) Our thoughts, words, and actions will be **judged** as to "what sort it is," namely "gold, silver, precious stones" or "wood, hay, stubble" (1 Corinthians 3:11-13) As Paul wrote, "if any man's work abide [the trying by fire]...he shall receive a reward." (1 Corinthians 3:14) But if our works yield nothing but smoke and ashes at the **judgment** we "shall suffer loss" of the rewards that could have been ours, yet be "saved...so as by fire." (1 Corinthians 3:15)

James continues explaining this future **judgment** of a believer's works. He writes that **he shall have** or receive **judgment without mercy, that have shewed no mercy**. On the one hand, the standard is most stringent. Yet on the other, it is one of **mercy**. Hodges' explanation here is right on target:

> Such is the solemnity of the Judgment Seat of Christ, however, that no man can view it without sensing how awesome and exacting it must be. Paul also sensed this feature of it (2 Cor 5:11). Any reasonable person must know that a judgment of his Christian life "by the book" (i.e., with full strictness) is likely to leave him with much censure from his Savior and with much loss of potential reward. What is needed in that day is *mercy*—a willingness on the part of our Lord and Judge to assess our words and deeds with the fullest possible measure of compassion... For if *the one who has shown no mercy* will experience none in that day, the converse must certainly be true: the one who has shown much mercy will experience much. Indeed, the mercy we show to others can actually "win the day" at that future experience of judgment, for *mercy triumphs over judgment*.[37]

---

[37] Zane C. Hodges, Arthur L. Farstad, and Robert N. Wilkin, *James*, 57–58.

How we live—how we carry out the royal law in our lives—will directly impact how our Lord examines and responds to our works and whether we receive rewards.

> **James 2:14** What *doth it* profit, my brethren, though a man say he hath faith, and have not works? can faith save him?

Now we come to the one of the most misunderstood verses in the New Testament. But it is not misunderstood because it is difficult. This verse is the poster child for theological commitments overriding the plain sense of the text. The confusion is a function of ignoring where this verse fits within the structure of the book, ignoring the immediate context of the verse, and assuming the wrong meanings of key words. Most commentaries on James attempt to exegete James 2:14 apart from the preceding verses with little attempt to defend their approach. But proper exegesis of this verse requires us to answer key questions based on the context: (1) what is being saved?; (2) saved from what?; and (3) what is the content of the **faith** under consideration?

We do well to first ground ourselves in the context. James writes in his thematic statement for the body of his epistle: "Wherefore, my beloved brethren, let every man be swift to hear, slow to speak, slow to wrath." (James 1:19) As I have indicated in the outline, James' key statement provides the overall organization of the main body of his epistle that follows, namely being swift to hear God's Word (1:21-2:26), being slow to speak (3:1-18), and being slow to wrath (4:1-5:6). Within the unit of thought on being swift to hear God's Word, James begins with the key principle and follows that with a thorough explanation: "Wherefore lay apart all filthiness and superfluity of naughtiness, and receive with meekness the engrafted word, which is able to save your souls." (James 1:21) James relates setting aside sin and humbly welcoming God's Word to the concept of saving our soul-lives (see notes on 1:21). As shown in the outline and in the preceding notes, James builds out the principle of 1:21 by distinguishing merely knowing God's Word from embracing and experiencing God's Word (1:22-27), providing a practical local church example where God's royal law is not being lived out because of partiality (2:1-7), and explaining that how well we live out the royal law (or perfect law of liberty) will be the standard of judgment of our Christian works (2:8-13). Now, James wants to emphasize that at the future judgment of our Christian works, knowing and believing God's Word will not be enough to save our soul-lives. Rather, James will argue, it is the "pure religion" of 1:27 that will save our soul-lives.

With this structural overview in mind, let's turn to the questions of what is being saved and from what. James asks the rhetorical question, **can faith save him?** James first used the word **save** in the first verse in this section (1:21). There, James said that "the engrafted word...is able to save your souls" or soul-lives. Having expounded on the other components of 1:21 but not specifically on the concept of saving our soul-lives, James now turns to that issue. He specifically references a **faith** that can **save him**. As shown in the notes for 1:21, our soul-lives refers to our temporal expression of life, and broadly speaking is comprised of our thoughts, words and actions, the very things that James indicates will be judged in 2:12-13. In this context, to speak of saving **him** is to speak of saving his soul-life, and this takes place at the judgment introduced in the prior two verses. It is in the immediate context of that future judgment "by the law of liberty" (2:12) where "mercy rejoiceth against judgment" (2:13) that James asks rhetorically, **can faith save him**, meaning, **can faith save him** at that judgment?

Some argue that 2:14 is about saving a person's physical life, but James never warns them that if they do not live right God will kill them. Others argue that James is addressing so-called spurious **faith** and that what he has in mind are fake believers who have mental assent in the facts of the gospel of Jesus Christ (death, burial, resurrection) but never truly believed. They argue that genuine (not spurious) **faith** must be demonstrated by works, and that James is saying here that these fake believers that never performed the requisite works are lost and going to hell. But James explains that the judgment in this context is exclusively a judgment of our works against the "law of liberty." In fact, everything about James 2 focuses on compliance with the royal law, and there is no reference in the entire epistle to the historic facts of the gospel. James repeatedly refers to his audience as "brethren" meaning fellow Christians. And this is why we must answer the fundamental question of what is the content of the **faith** under consideration in 2:14. Expositors advocating the spurious **faith** theory almost always simply assume it is **faith** in the gospel of Jesus Christ, but that cannot be supported by the text.

Remember, we are in a unit focused on the principle of being "swift to hear" (1:19). James introduces the concept in 1:21 that we should welcome God's Word, "which is able to save your souls," and then immediately follows that up with discussion about being "doers of the word, and not hearers only" (1:22), looking "into the perfect law of liberty, and continueth therein" (1:25), visiting widows and orphans (1:27), not showing partiality in the local church (2:1-7), fulfilling the royal law of loving our neighbors (2:8-12), and then being judged according to the royal law / law of liberty (2:12-13). It is unfortunate that many readers *assume* when they see the word **faith** that the content is necessarily the gospel. The context here demands that the content of **faith** under examination is not the gospel, but God's Word in general, as exemplified by the royal law / law of liberty. James' interest is not getting his audience saved from sin's penalty, but "saving the saved" at the coming judgment by getting Christians to live out God's Word in their daily lives. Moreover, he previously referenced **faith** in several verses. (James 1:3, 6, 2:1, and 2:5) As previously shown in the notes, James uses **faith** to indicate trusting in God's provision or His Word in general. Nothing in the context of the prior usages suggests that James is looking at **faith** in the gospel of Jesus Christ.

As Christians, we need to recognize that the content of **faith** in the Bible is frequently not the gospel, but is often God's Word or apostolic doctrine. This is well-illustrated by Hebrews 11:1: "Now faith is the substance of things hoped for, the evidence of things not seen." The writer of Hebrews describes what **faith** looks like in the Christian walk. He especially has in mind God's promised future blessings, and what he says is that if we believe (have **faith** in) what God says about the future ("things hoped for"), we will reorient out lives around it today. In that sense, our lives become "evidence of things not seen" because our lives reflect what we claim to believe. Most of the examples in the hall of faith in Hebrews 11 exemplify this principle, showing us believers of the past that reoriented their lives around God's promises about the future. Noah built the ark because God warned him of a future flood. Abraham left his home for the Promise Land based on God's promised future blessings there. To use the language of James, they were doers and not hearers only.

Turning back to James 2:14, he asks rhetorically, **can faith save him?** In other words, **can** believing God's Word **save** at the judgment of 2:12-13? And in particular, **can** merely believing the royal law / law of liberty **save** a soul-life at the judgment of a Christian's works according to the standard set forth in the law of liberty? The answer demanded is no because the standard requires obedience, not just belief that the command to love others is from God. James asks, **what doeth it profit** or benefit, **my brethren** or fellow Christians, **though a man say he hath faith** or believes the royal law, **and have not works?** If there were any lingering question as to the content of this **faith**, they are answered unequivocally in the verses that follow.

James' first illustration supporting 2:14 is a hypothetical where a Christian has opportunity but fails to live out the royal law by providing food and clothing to another destitute Christian (2:16). James is not talking about whether someone really trusted Christ for the forgiveness of sins; he is talking about the royal law (and more generally God's Word, for which the royal law is a fitting proxy). James faces the same problem we have in our churches today. Everyone agrees we are supposed to love God and love others, but how many are genuinely living out that truth day by day. And the warning is NOT that unloving people are fake Christians. The warning is that being a hearer only of God's Word will be no benefit at the judgment. And why is that? Because the judgment determines whether we just heard (believed) the royal law or humbly welcomed it as God's implanted word, so that like a seed it germinated and produced good works in our lives.

Finally, before we proceed with the balance of the chapter, we have seen how critical understanding the structure of the book of James is to proper exegesis. The verses that follow have suffered from a lack of appreciation of the structure. The key is seeing that James uses two inclusios to illustrate the relationship between **faith** in God's Word and living out God's Word. An inclusio is a cohesive unit of thought that is bracketed at the beginning and ending with similar phrases. Both inclusios begin and end with references to **faith** and **works**. The first inclusio is James 2:14-17; note how 2:14 and 2:17 both reference **faith** and **works**.[38] The second inclusio is James 2:20-26, and again the first and last verses of the inclusio reference **faith** and **works**. Between the two inclusios is a diatribe against a hypothetical objector (2:18-20) that many readers fail to recognize. The highly organized structure of this last subsection (2:14-26) within the larger unit (1:21-2:26) helps us see how it all fits together. We are able to see how James expounded his key principle in 1:21 one piece at a time, and this last subsection (2:14-26) is all about the matter of the relationship between God's Word, our works, and saving our soul-lives at the bema judgment.

> **James 2:15** If a brother or sister be naked, and destitute of daily food, **16** And one of you say unto them, Depart in peace, be *ye* warmed and filled; notwithstanding ye give

---

[38] Kenneth M. Wilson, "Reading James 2:18-20 With Anti-Donatist Eyes: Untangling Augustine's Exegetical Legacy," *Journal of Biblical Literature* 139, no. 2 (2020), 400

them not those things which are needful to the body; what *doth it* profit? 17 Even so faith, if it hath not works, is dead, being alone.

These three verses comprise the first faith-works inclusio (2:14-17) with as practical an illustration as James could possibly provide. He presents a simple hypothetical of a **brother or sister**, meaning a fellow Christian, in need. This **brother or sister** is **naked, and destitute of daily food**. To be **naked** indicates such poverty that this person's clothing is either completely tattered and falling apart, or that this person is wearing makeshift clothing. In the United States today, quality clothing is rather inexpensive, but it was not that long ago in this country that poor people used potato sacks and other similar means to make clothing for their children. In the ancient world, nice clothing was a luxury and most people did not have a closet of clothing to choose from. This person also does not know where their next meal is coming from.

The hypothetical assumes that **one of you** is fully able to provide this Christian **brother or sister** with both clothes and food but instead says **unto them, Depart in peace, be ye warmed and filled**. To paraphrase, "I love you and I will be praying for you." But **notwithstanding ye give them not those things which are needful to the body**. In the hypothetical, the words in isolation sound caring, reflecting a Christian that knows the royal law, but the royal law has not been humbly welcomed as God's implanted word. The poor **brother or sister** is turned away without meeting their needs. And the rhetorical question is, **what doth it profit?** In other words, what will knowing and believing the royal law profit **one of you** at the judgment if you failed to actually love this **brother or sister** by providing what they needed. Remember, you "shall have judgment without mercy, that hath shewed no mercy." (James 2:13)

James now closes the first faith-works inclusio with the key principle: **even so faith, if it hath not works, is dead, being alone.** Obviously, James is not speaking of a spurious **faith** in the gospel of Christ. Rather, he is saying, **even so faith** in the royal law, **if it hath not works, is dead, being alone.** With this statement James introduces the word **dead** which he has not previously used. As with **faith,** "save," and "soul," people tend to apply a definition of **dead** based on their theological commitment, rather than a lexical meaning that fits the context. The term **dead** can obviously refer to physical death, but that does not work here because the hypothetical Christian is alive and able to tell the poor **brother or sister** to **depart in peace.** The term can also be used figuratively, as Hodges explains:

> As a metaphor, *dead* is often treated as though it could refer to nothing other than the death/life terminology employed to describe salvation from hell. But every linguist knows that "death" and "deadness" are concepts that have given rise to numerous and diverse metaphors in nearly every language. English itself has many ("this law's a dead letter," "you're dead wrong," "he's dead drunk," "he's a dead duck," "that idea is dead," "they navigated by dead reckoning," etc.). So also the Greek language (and the NT itself) abounds in such metaphors.[39]

---

[39] Zane C. Hodges, Arthur L. Farstad, and Robert N. Wilkin, *James*, 62–63.

Such figurative uses abound in the New Testament. For example, we see figurative uses in Romans 4:19 where Abraham "considered his own body now dead, when he was about an hundred years old, neither yet the deadness of Sara's womb." The word "dead" and "deadness" obviously did not mean physically dead nor nonexistent. Rather, Abraham was physically impotent and his wife Sara was barren. The idea of death is figurative for *useless* or *unproductive* but not *nonexistent*. We see another figurative use in Romans 7:8 where Paul writes about his own experience and states that "without the law sin was dead." Certainly Paul did not mean that "sin" was nonexistent in his life (i.e., that he is sinless) before he understood the "law." His point is his personal unawareness of sin until he knew the law. The author of Hebrews refers to "not laying again the foundation of repentance of dead works, and of faith toward God" (Hebrews 6:1) and does not mean spurious works or nonexistent works, but works that are useless in the context of justification, which is through faith. (see also Hebrews 9:14, "dead works") There are numerous other examples of figurative uses that do not mean anything like fake, spurious, or nonexistent. (e.g., Matthew 8:22; Romans 6:11, 8:10; Ephesians 2:1, 2:5; Colossians 2:13; Revelation 3:1)

When James concludes his first faith-works inclusio with the statement that **faith, if it hath not works, is dead, being alone**, he means by **dead** that this kind of **faith** is useless or non-beneficial at the judgment. This relates back to the first verse of the inclusio where James writes, "What doth is profit" or benefit you, "my brethren, though a man say he hath faith, and have not works? Can faith save him?" As throughout the entire larger section of thought (1:21-2:26), the issue is humbly embracing God's

Word with a view to living it out faithfully. Being a hearer (believer) of God's Word, but not a doer, will not cut it at the judgment of 2:12-13. A **faith** that believes God's Word but does not humbly embrace it and live it out is useless. It was useless to the hypothetical **brother or sister** in need, and it is useless at the coming judgment according to the law of liberty—it will not save or deliver the soul-life in the sense of receiving rewards from Jesus.

> **James 2:18** Yea, a man may say, Thou hast faith, and I have works: shew me thy faith without thy works, and I will shew thee my faith by my works. **19** Thou believest that there is one God; thou doest well: the devils also believe, and tremble. **20** But wilt thou know, O vain man, that faith without works is dead?

Between the two inclusios (2:14-17 and 2:21-26) James employs a common ancient literary device called a diatribe. A diatribe presents a hypothetical objection from a hypothetical objector (called an interlocutor) and then makes an abrupt retort. This passage was misinterpreted by Augustine based on a faulty Latin translation, and then many in the Reform tradition continued his error.[40] The passage suffers from expositors almost unanimously ignoring the larger context of 1:21-2:26, failing to recognize that the diatribe is nestled between two inclusios, ignoring ancient textual conventions concerning how a diatribe is structured, and modern translations imposing theological commitments to the diatribe when they misplace the quotation marks

---

[40] Kenneth M. Wilson, "Reading James 2:18-20 With Anti-Donatist Eyes: Untangling Augustine's Exegetical Legacy," 386-387.

around who is speaking. The disputed issue is who is talking in each phrase, James or the interlocutor.

Kenneth Wilson explains the structure of a diatribe in the ancient Greek literature:

> Stanley K. Stowers demonstrated that interlocutor conventions in the Greek New Testament share structural characteristics with classical Greek diatribes. Authors introduced their diatribes with, 'someone will say' or 'you say to me.' The interlocutor's words follow. Authors signaled a return to their own words with, 'but will you not know,' 'O vain man,' or similar adversative or pejorative indicators.[41]

We find two clear New Testament examples of diatribes in Romans 9:19-20 and 1 Corinthians 15:35-36. Notice below how these diatribes reflect the key elements found in classical Greek diatribes: (1) an introduction like "someone will say," (2) the interlocutor's argument, and (3) an obvious adversative or pejorative signal that the author is now responding to the interlocutor.

> (1) But some *man* will say, (2) How are the dead raised up? and with what body do they come? (3) *Thou* fool, that which thou sowest is not quickened, except it die. (1 Corinthians 15:35-36)

> (1) Thou wilt say then unto me, (2) Why doth he yet find fault? For who hath resisted his will? Nay but, O man, who art

---

[41] Ibid., 386.

thou that repliest against God? Shall the
thing formed say to him that formed *it*,
Why hast thou made me thus? (3) Nay but,
O man, who art thou that repliest against
God? Shall the thing formed say to him that
formed *it*, Why hast thou made me thus?
(Romans 9:19-20)

James follows the standard diatribe pattern, introducing
the interlocutor's objection in 2:18 (**Yea, a man may say**)
and then signaling his response with a pejorative (**O vain
man**) in 2:20. This demonstrates that the dialogue
preceding the pejorative is solely the words of the
objector. The substance of that dialogue validates what
we should expect from the diatribe structure, namely that
the words do not represent James' thoughts but the
interlocutor's. The interlocutor first states his objection:
**Thou has faith, and I have works: shew me thy faith
without thy works, and I will show thee my faith by my
works.** I pause here to note that most expositors argue
that James responds with **shew me thy faith without thy
works, and I will show thee my faith by my works.** But if
this were the case, then the entire objection would be,
Thou has faith, and I have works, which is both
incomplete and unsubstantiated. It is evident that this is
only half of the interlocutor's argument, which has driven
some commentators to ignore the diatribe altogether and
attribute the entire dialogue to James. But that position
makes the diatribe introduction and pejorative response
to the **vain man** nonsensical.

Returning to the interlocutor's objection, his thesis is that
there is no relationship between **faith** and **works**. He
argues his point in 2:18 then supports it with an

illustration in 2:19. Arguing his position, he says, **shew me thy faith without my works, and I will shew thee my faith by my works.** At this point, many (probably most) attribute to James the words, **I will shew thee my faith by my works.** This not only makes the interlocutor's argument incomplete, but it violates the standard diatribe pattern. This position derives from a theological commitment to the concept of fake or spurious faith. What is missed is that both alternatives, (1) **shew me thy faith without my works** and (2) **I will shew thee my faith by my works**, are logical impossibilities.[42] No one disputes that **works** might evidence **faith**, but faithless people may emulate good **works.** The point of the interlocutor's argument is that both alternatives are obviously impossible, and because faith cannot be proven with or without works, **faith** and **works** are independent. Wilson summarizes well: "No human can see faith; humans only see works. It is impossible for James to demonstrate his faith to the objector with or without works; or, for the interlocutor to show his faith by his works (2:18). Even non-Christians have good works without faith."[43]

The interlocutor then provides an illustration that **faith** is independent of **works.** He states, **Thou believest that there is one God; thou doest well: the devils also believe, and tremble.** Here again, almost all expositors attribute these words to James, contravening the diatribe pattern. They see James employing sarcasm with the words **thou doest well,** understanding them like "good for you that you believe that," but make little or no effort to prove their position. The Greek phrase καλῶς ποιεῖς· (kalōs

---

[42] Ibid., 400-401.
[43] Ibid., 400.

poieis) translated **thou doest well** also occurs in James 2:8 ("If ye fulfil the royal law...**ye do well**") and no one suggests it means anything other than an affirmation that if they fulfill the royal law they are doing right by God. As Wilson observes:

> James 1:23, 1:25, 2:12, and 3:18 similarly use ποιέω (or cognates) in the context of being good. In fact, the modern pejorative or sarcastic meaning "good for you" for καλῶς ποιεῖς· cannot be identified anywhere in the early Greek literature. In contrast, all New Testament and Septuagint passage using καλῶς ποιεῖν match the meaning "to do good [works/live well]."[44]

These are not James' words or sarcasm. The interlocutor illustrates his thesis by referencing the *shema* from Deuteronomy 6:4: "Hear, O Israel: The LORD our God is one LORD." It is to be noted that if James' concern was spurious believers (aka fake Christians) he would be talking about the gospel, not posing an interlocutor objection about the *shema*. The interlocutor means to demonstrate the independence of **faith** and **works**. As previously noted, the **faith** at issue is not believing the gospel, but generally **faith** in or believing God's Word. Thus, he says, **thou believest** [the verb form of **faith**] **that there is one God; thou doest well**. In other words, you believe the *shema*—monotheism—and as a result you do good works. But **the devils also believe** that there is only one God, and instead of doing good works, they **tremble**. This shows **faith** and **works** are unrelated. I would also note here that the idea of **devils** having **faith** is not taught anywhere else in the Bible,

---

44 Ibid., 399.

making it highly improbable these could be James' words. Rather, they are intended to show a certain overreaching on the part of the interlocutor. We will see that James prefers well-known Old Testament illustrations for his Jewish Christian readers.

James signals his rejoinder with the pejorative, **But will thou know, O vain man**. James responds with a rhetorical question that begins the second and longer faith-works inclusio (2:20-26). He asks, don't you **know...that faith without works is dead?** What confuses some readers is that James responds to the interlocutor, but does not directly answer his objection. Throughout the present unit of thought that started in 1:21, James emphasizes being a doer of the Word and not merely a hearer (believer) of the Word. The interlocutor's argument about the independence of **faith** and **works** is a direct objection to James exhortation that they need to be doers of the Word. The interlocutor's unstated conclusion is that **works** are unnecessary in the life of a Christian. Being a hearer—knowing the truth—is good enough. James' rhetorical question is a response to that unstated conclusion. James' point is that good **works** are necessary at the coming judgment seat of Christ. And just as the interlocutor appeals to an illustration, albeit not one found elsewhere in the Bible, James will appeal to two well-known Old Testament illustrations in the verses that follow. What James does not say in response to the interlocutor undermines the position taken by most expositors. "Note well that James does not respond 'demons have the wrong type of faith,' or 'good works inevitably follow true faith,' or even dispute that works cannot prove faith, as commentaries ubiquitously assume."[45]

---

[45] Ibid., 402.

James 2:21 Was not Abraham our father justified by works, when he had offered Isaac his son upon the altar? **22** Seest thou how faith wrought with his works, and by works was faith made perfect? **23** And the scripture was fulfilled which saith, Abraham believed God, and it was imputed unto him for righteousness: and he was called the Friend of God. **24** Ye see then how that by works a man is justified, and not by faith only.

Within his longer faith-works inclusio (2:20-26), James argues that Christian **works** are necessary for the coming judgment by appealing to two well-known Old Testament examples from the lives of **Abraham** and Rahab. He asks, **was not Abraham our father justified by works, when he had offered Isaac his son upon the altar?** Some have seen a contradiction between James 2:21 and Paul's argument in Romans 4 that **Abraham was** not **justified by works.** The problem is that we have developed a theological understanding of the term **justified** as Paul uses it in Romans—that God declares us righteous (justifies us) when we respond in faith to the gospel. But the Greek word δικαιόω (*dikaioō*) means "to render a favorable verdict, *vindicate.*"[46] In Romans 4, **Abraham** was vindicated before God through his **faith** and only God can see that **faith.** But James has in mind, as he has from 1:21 to this point, works, including what others see and hear. James thus speaks of Abraham's vindication before men or his public, visible vindication. His rhetorical question demands an affirmative

---

46 William Arndt et al., *A Greek-English Lexicon of the New Testament and Other Early Christian Literature* (Chicago: University of Chicago Press, 2000), 249.

answer, **Abraham** was **justified by works** publicly **when he...offered Isaac his son upon the altar**. And it is this kind of vindication that will matter at the bema.

James explains, **seest thou how faith wrought with his works, and by works was faith made perfect** or complete? He appeals to Genesis 15:6 when he writes that **the scripture was fulfilled, which saith, Abraham believed God, and it was imputed unto him for righteousness**. Paul appeals to the same verse in Romans 4, but for a different purpose. Here, James links Genesis 15:6 to Abraham's subsequent offering of **Isaac his son upon the altar** in Genesis 22, decades later. If we did not have more from James, we might find a contradiction. But James adds, **and** Abraham **was called the Friend of God**. (see 2 Chronicles 20:7; Isaiah 41:8) The **faith** that **Abraham** placed in God's promises in Genesis 15:6 matured or completed (**made perfect**) over time, and in that sense, his **faith** first mentioned in Genesis 15:6 is visibly vindicated in Genesis 22 in the works produced from his **faith** that God would provide him an heir, and indeed, a great lineage. (Genesis 15:4-5) The episode in Genesis 22 put Abraham's belief in what God told him in Genesis 15:4-5 to the test. Harry Leafe's analysis is helpful:

> Every believer in Christ has faith, but it is what is produced by that faith that gives it its reality and value. There is no better example of that than of Abraham offering his son, Isaac, as a sacrifice (2:21-24). Abraham had faith. God had earlier proclaimed him righteous on the basis of it – apart from any works whatsoever (Gen. 15:6; Rom. 4:1-25). Now, many years later, in

the providence of God, he is being placed in a situation where his faith is to be "proven."

Abraham's son, Isaac, was the individual through whom God would confirm the covenant. He was the only son of promise. What would Abraham do? How would he reason? Would his evaluation of himself and his circumstances issue from faith in the revelation of God? Would his thoughts, words and actions *prove* the *character* of his faith?[47]

Abraham's offering of **Isaac his son upon the altar** is the work that resulted from Abraham humbly embracing God's Word back in Genesis 15. His was *proven faith*. As we read in Hebrews 11:17-19: "By faith Abraham, when he was tried, offered up Isaac: and he that had received the promises offered up his only begotten *son*, Of whom it was said, That in Isaac shall thy seed be called: Accounting that God *was* able to raise *him* up, even from the dead; from whence also he received him in a figure."

> **James 2:25** Likewise also was not Rahab the harlot justified by works, when she had received the messengers, and had sent *them* out another way? **26** For as the body without the spirit is dead, so faith without works is dead also.

James next illustrates his point that works are necessary at the coming judgment by appealing to the example of **Rahab the harlot** in Joshua 2. Like Abraham, she also was

---

[47] G. Harry Leafe, *Running to Win!*, 23-24.

99

justified or visibly vindicated before men **by works**, and that is what matters at the judgment. She was **justified by works when she...received the messengers** or spies in Jericho and protected them from capture by sending them **out** of the city **another way**. She fulfilled the royal law to the spies.

James now brings his second inclusio to completion with a repeat of his initial response to the interlocutor in 2:20 (don't you "know...that faith without works is dead?"). He writes affirmatively, **For as the body without the spirit is dead, so faith without works is dead also.** Our physical **body** is useless **without** our **spirit** because God made us a unity of the material and immaterial and our body can only function in the context of this unity. In the same way, in reference to the coming judgment of our works (the judgment seat of Christ), **faith without works** is useless. We should follow the examples of Abraham and **Rahab** whose **faith** in God and His Word produced good **works**.

Closing

The quality of a diamond is measured based on the quality of the cut (does it sparkle well?), the color (the less color the better), clarity (no imperfections), and carat (weight). Many a person has taken a diamond ring to a jeweler to have it appraised and certified based on the four C's for grading diamonds. The issue is not whether it is really a diamond, but the quality of the diamond. That is how it is with our faith in God's Word. We will stand before Jesus and give an account, not with a view to whether we had faith or whether we are a Christian. The issue is the quality of our faith in God's Word as demonstrated by how we lived—and especially how we lived out the command to love God and others.

Someone may at this point suggest they have no concern about this future judgment. After all, all they care about is that they will be in heaven someday, and in any event, they should not do good works because of a motivation to get a reward. But Jesus' command to lay up treasure in heaven is exactly that—a command. And James' admonition to be a doer of the Word like Abraham and Rahab is a command. Life is serious business and standing before Jesus with nothing to show for our lives, even if we try to dress our disobedience in pious garbs, makes us like the servant of Luke 19:20-24 that hid his pound and disobeyed his master about serving until he returns. We will care when we stand before the Lord. At that moment there will be no excuses, just the reality of how we chose to live our life—did we squander it on worldly pursuits or did we live a life rich toward God? The day will show the quality of our faith.

Application Points

Main Principle: Christians need to live out God's Word in their daily lives, including especially the royal law that we love God and love our neighbors, knowing that the quality of our faith in God's Word will be judged by the Lord, and that our soul-lives will be delivered at that judgment in the form of receiving rewards only to the extent that our faith produced Christian good works. (This judgment is not about whether we believed the gospel and where we will spend eternity.)

Discussion Questions

1. What are different ways people may show partiality in local churches? Why is it wrong?

2. What is the royal law? Can you think of any sin that could be committed against another person that does not violate the royal law?

3. James says to speak and act as those that will be judged. If all of our speech will be judged by Jesus, what are the implications for how we ought to speak to others? Or about others? How does this apply to our speech in social media platforms like Facebook?

4. Why would a Christian fail (or refuse) to live out their faith, including the royal law?

5. What are the rewards Jesus gives at the judgment?

6. Should Christians be motivated by the prospect of receiving rewards from Jesus?

7. Should Christians be concerned about the coming judgment?

8. What would a Christian's life look like before other people if at the judgment he or she gets zero rewards? (see 1 Corinthians 3:15)

Chapter 5

Our Words Matter

James 3:1-18

We are the master of our words until we utter them. Once they are out, they take on a life of their own, and sometimes they cannot be stopped. Words can be forgiven, but are rarely forgotten. Our words can build people up and tear them down. Encouragement and praise can empower people, but accusations, even false ones, can destroy a person's livelihood and reputation and even end their life. The Bible says a great deal about how Christians ought to speak, including speech that we should never use like gossip and slander. Yet how easily we find it to speak hate and death instead of life and peace. Technology has brought new means of communications, like social media, and with these innovations, new avenues for abusive speech. It should be no small matter to us that we will all stand before the Lord and account for every word, including what we say on social media. Perhaps the most profound truth that James gives us about our speech is how it reveals our level of spiritual maturity.

Outline

I. GREETING (1:1)

II. GOD USES TESTS AND TRIALS TO GROW US
    TO MATURITY (1:1-18)

III. **CENTRAL EXHORTATION:** THE CHRISTIAN
     GROWING TO MATURITY IS QUICK TO
     HEAR, SLOW TO SPEAK AND SLOW TO
     ANGER (1:19-20)

IV. GOOD HEARERS HUMBLY EMBRACE GOD'S
    IMPLANTED WORD AND LIVE IT OUT TO
    THE SAVING OF THE SOUL-LIFE AT THE
    JUDGMENT (1:21-2:26)

V. BE SLOW TO SPEAK BECAUSE YOUR
    WORDS WILL BE JUDGED AND HOW YOU
    SPEAK REVEALS YOUR MATURITY AND
    THE WISDOM YOU LIVE BY (3:1-18)

   a. **Key Principle About Being Slow to Speak**: Be
      wise about becoming a teacher of God's Word
      because you will be subject to a stricter judgment.
      (3:1)

   b. Controlling our speech is a hallmark of spiritual
      maturity and indicates disciplined control over
      our entire body (works). (3:2-4)

      i.   Illustrated by the use of a small bit to control
           the entire horse's body. (3:3)

      ii. Illustrated by the use of a small rudder to
           control the entire ship. (3:4)

      iii. Negatively illustrated by a small fire the
           scorches an entire forest. (3:5)

  iv. Lack of control of our speech will pollute our entire body (works). (3:6)

 c. Our speech cannot be completely controlled. (3:7-12)

  i. Contrasted with animals that can be tamed. (3:7)

  ii. Our speech cannot be completely controlled because it is corrupted. (3:8-10)

  iii. The incongruity of uncontrolled speech illustrated by a spring of water, a fig tree, and a grape vine. (3:11-12)

 d. Our speech is a reflection of the wisdom we choose to live by. (3:13-18)

  i. Our Christian works show we are living in humility that derives from heavenly wisdom. (3:13)

  ii. But boasting and lying shows selfish ambition in our hearts that derives from worldly, demonic wisdom. (3:14-16)

  iii. Heavenly wisdom lived out produces godly thinking and the fruit of righteousness and peace with one another. (3:17-18)

Scripture and Comments

Self-control over our speech is so important to our walk with the Lord that James addresses it in all five chapters of his epistle. We need to be "quick to hear" what James has to say about speech.

James 3:1 My brethren, be not many masters, knowing that we shall receive the greater condemnation.

With this verse, James begins the second major unit of material (3:1-18) within the main body of his epistle. The verse serves as a transition because it specifically addresses the judgment of believers' works that was central to the first major unit of material (1:21-2:26) and reintroduces the issue of the believer's speech. Recall first that the three major units of material (1:21-2:26; 3:1-18; 4:1-5:6) build out James' central exhortation from 1:19: "Wherefore, my beloved brethren, let every man be swift to hear, slow to speak, slow to wrath." Recall also that James already stated one of his key principles about speech in 1:26: "If any man among you seem to be religious, and bridleth not his tongue, but deceiveth his own heart, this man's religion *is* vain." This last point he will return to in the immediately succeeding verses.

James knows his audience, and he is apparently aware that too many people are stepping forward as **masters** (Gr. *didaskalos*, teachers) but do not yet have the maturity they should have to be teachers. His concern should also be understood against the backdrop of the early church practice of letting multiple people speak when they gathered rather than having one designated speaker as most churches do today. James writes that they should **be not many masters** or teachers. Teaching in this context is publicly speaking about God and His Word, a matter to be taken up with the greatest care. I think the person who steps up to teach or preach needs to have something from the Bible to say, care about his or her audience, and have humility. From the balance of James 3, it appears these elements were missing.

Teaching should not be taken lightly because teachers **shall receive the greater condemnation**. The word translated **condemnation** is James' only use of the word κρίμα (krima), which in this context BDAG defines as "legal decision rendered by a judge, *judicial verdict*."[48] In the immediate context, the judgment is that judgment of James 2:12-13 that is at issue throughout the first major unit in 1:21-2:26. As the prior notes indicate, this works judgment for believers is with a view to rewards and is what many refer to as the bema judgment or judgment seat of Christ. But why is it a **greater** or stricter standard of judgment for teachers? It is because they hold themselves out as having a greater knowledge of God's Word. Their words and conduct should reflect that greater knowledge: "So speak ye, and so do, as they that shall be judged by the law of liberty." (2:12)

In the role as teacher, we need to understand that what we say will be judged ("so speak ye") as well as our obedience to our understanding of God's Word ("and so do"). If we misrepresent God's Word we should expect a **greater** (stricter) judgment. If we correctly teach God's Word but do not obey what we know or claim to know about God's Word, we are hypocrites. And because we as teachers should know better, we will face the **greater** judgment at the bema. We should never take the role of teacher—whether it is in the pulpit or some less formal role—lightly. We should not be slothful in our preparation, dilatory in our speaking about God's Word, or hypocritical in our failure to model it before those we teach. Surely at the heart of what James is addressing is

---

[48] William Arndt et al., *A Greek-English Lexicon of the New Testament and Other Early Christian Literature*, 567.

humility. Christians who teach should reflect a level of spiritual maturity in their lives. Teaching God's Word is not about feeding your ego, but edifying others. Prideful people are all too willing to speak when they need to spend more time listening. Remember that a call to preach or teach the Bible is a call to preparation.

One final note is that while James addresses the speech of teachers specifically, the reality that God will judge our words at the bema was already stated (2:12) and the material that follows in the balance of James 3 surely has application to all of us as we think about our speech.

> **James 3:2** For in many things we offend all. If any man offend not in word, the same *is* a perfect man, *and* able also to bridle the whole body. **3** Behold, we put bits in the horses' mouths, that they may obey us; and we turn about their whole body. **4** Behold also the ships, which though *they be* so great, and *are* driven of fierce winds, yet are they turned about with a very small helm, whithersoever the governor listeth.

James previously noted that the ability to control our speech is a hallmark of spiritual maturity. (James 1:26) That principle is now re-stated, then built out and illustrated both positively and negatively. James writes that **in many things we offend all**, meaning that we all sin in **many** ways. The word translated **offend** is the Greek πταίω (*ptaiō*), which literally means to trip or stumble, a figurative way to refer to our sin. None of us are perfect, but **if any man offend** (stumble) **not in word** or speech, **the same is a perfect** or mature **man, and able also to bridle** or control **the whole body**. A Christian that can control his or her speech has control over their whole person, and for this reason the ability to control speech is a hallmark of spiritual maturity. By the same token, our words will betray our lack of maturity as well.

James now illustrates the principle in 3:2 positively with two illustrations. First, controlling our tongue, the physical member that enables our speech, is illustrated by how a small bit controls a large horse. For **if we put bits into the horses' mouths, that they may obey us; and we turn about their whole body**. A large horse can be controlled and directed by pulling the reigns that pull the small **bits** in their **mouths**. In the same way, if we can control our "bit" (our tongue) we can direct our **whole body**.

Similarly, **ships**, despite their **great** size, being **driven of fierce** or harsh **winds, are...turned about** or controlled **with a very small helm** (the rudder), **whithersoever the governor** (pilot) **listeth**. It is any easy exercise to find photographs on the internet of ship rudders. Even a large military aircraft carrier has a rudder that is small in comparison to the overall size of the ship, and that rudder causes the entire ship to turn one direction or the other. In the same way, our tongue is small in comparison to our **whole body** but if we have control of our rudder (our tongue and thus our speech) we can direct our ship. This is a critical mark of maturity and I fear that most Christians do not understand this principle.

> **James 3:5** Even so the tongue is a little member, and boasteth great things. Behold, how great a matter a little fire kindleth! **6** And the tongue *is* a fire, a world of iniquity: so is the tongue among our members, that it defileth the whole body,

and setteth on fire the course of nature; and
it is set on fire of hell.

James now provides negative illustrations about the
potential damage that may be caused by our speech. The
old saying is true, you cannot un-ring the bell. We lose all
control over the words once they leave our mouths. Even
sincere apologies may not undo the negative consequences
of our speech, which can be severe and permanent.

First, James points out that while **the tongue is a little
member** relative to the rest of our body, it **boasteth great
things**. The Bible frequently associates boastful speech
with evil people. Of the anti-Christ, the Bible says he has
"a mouth speaking great things," a point emphasized in
Daniel 7:8, 20 and 25, as well as Revelation 13:5-6. Likewise,
the false prophet that causes people to worship anti-Christ
"had two horns like a lamb" but "he spake as a dragon."
(Revelation 13:11) Similarly, we are warned about the
speech of false prophets and teachers. (Matthew 7:20) It is
a beneficial exercise to walk through the book of Jude and
mark every instance where speech is addressed. (Jude 4
"denying the only Lord God, and our Lord Jesus Christ"; 8
"speak evil of dignities"; 10 "these speak evil of those
things they know not"; 11 "ran greedily after the error of
Balaam for reward" who prophesied falsely for money; 15
"their hard speeches which ungodly sinners have spoken
against them"; 16 "murmurers, complainers...their mouth
speaketh great swelling words"; 18 "mockers")

James calls upon his readers to **behold** or consider **how
great a matter a little fire kindleth**. The word **matter**
translates the Greek ὕλη (*hule*) and means a forest. We all
know from common experience that the smallest spark at
the right time can cause a fire that burns hundreds or

thousands of acres of forest land. In relatively recent news such fires were started from a discarded cigarette and pyrotechnics used at a gender reveal party, and severe but unintended devastation followed. That is the picture here. As the small and seemingly inconsequential spark can set ablaze and destroy a **great** forest, so also our words can be that spark that causes great devastation in people's lives. Because **the tongue is a fire**, how we handle our speech is extraordinarily important. Those who own handguns know the first rule of handguns—always assume they are loaded. We recognize how dangerous a firearm can be and so ownership comes with responsibilities in how we handle a firearm. The same is true of our **tongue** because it is always loaded with the potential irreversible damage.

The **tongue** represents **a world of iniquity** because while we can use any of our members to carry out the sin that lurks in our hearts, all of that iniquity can proceed from our speech. Hear Jesus' words in this regard:

> **Matthew 12:34** O generation of vipers, how can ye, being evil, speak good things? for out of the abundance of the heart the mouth speaketh. **35** A good man out of the good treasure of the heart bringeth forth good things: and an evil man out of the evil treasure bringeth forth evil things. **36** But I say unto you, That every idle word that men shall speak, they shall give account thereof in the day of judgment. **37** For by thy words thou shalt be justified, and by thy words thou shalt be condemned.

> **Matthew 15:17** Do not ye yet understand, that whatsoever entereth in at the mouth

> goeth into the belly, and is cast out into the draught? **18** But those things which proceed out of the mouth come forth from the heart; and they defile the man. **19** For out of the heart proceed evil thoughts, murders, adulteries, fornications, thefts, false witness, blasphemies: **20** These are *the things* which defile a man: but to eat with unwashen hands defileth not a man.

As Jesus said in Matthew 15:20, what comes out of our mouths **defileth the whole body, and setteth on fire the course of nature**. Just as those who can control their **tongue** can control their whole person, so also when we let our **tongue** out of control it defiles our whole person, releasing iniquity that burns everything in our way like an invading army. The destruction is **set on fire of** or by **hell**. Here, the word **hell** is the Greek γέεννα (*geena*), a word of Jewish origin that referred to the valley of Hinnom in Jerusalem, which figuratively may be used of "hell" because it came to be a place where the rubbish was burned. The point is that such wicked speech is sourced in **hell** itself. James will address the fact that our speech reflects the wisdom we live by, either the heavenly (3:13, 17-18) or demonic (3:14-16). Christians bring hell's fire on earth when they allow their tongues to pour out **fire**.

We must pause and be sure we do not see this as mere academics. Controlling our speech is probably the most difficult part of the Christian walk. Our words are the assault weapons of choice for Christians. How many married believers have burned one another to a cinder with words? How many churches went to war over poorly chosen words? We can speak evil with uncontrolled tenacity and havoc and I have repeatedly witnessed this in a church context from Christians who think themselves godly and mature. Jesus is listening.

> **James 3:7** For every kind of beasts, and of birds, and of serpents, and of things in the sea, is tamed, and hath been tamed of mankind: **8** But the tongue can no man tame; *it is* an unruly evil, full of deadly poison.

We need to understand that controlling the tongue is no easy matter. James illustrates with animals, who can relatively easily be subdued or tamed—**every kind of beasts, and of birds, and of serpents, and of things in the sea, is tamed, and hath been tamed of mankind.** We think highly of ourselves because of our perception of our own accomplishments. (cf. Nebuchadnezzar in Daniel 4:28-31) Humanity can tame animals of all sorts. Yet taming **the tongue** eludes us. James says **the tongue can no man tame** because **it is an unruly evil, full of deadly poison.** It is interesting that James notes that **serpents** can be subdued, some of which are venomous. But the **tongue** is never fully subdued and is **full of deadly poison** like a venomous snake.

Akin to saying the **tongue** is a fire, saying it has **deadly poison** means our words may speak life or death. As we read in Proverbs 18:21: "Death and life *are* in the power of the tongue: and they that love it shall eat the fruit thereof." (see also Proverbs 25:11-13) One particularly **deadly** type of speech is gossip, which the Proverbs condemn. (Proverbs 11:13, 26:20-24) Another is slander. (Proverbs 10:18, 20:19) The apostle Paul was cognizant of the dangers of the **tongue** and said we should only speak words that will edify: "Let no corrupt communication proceed out of your mouth, but that which is good to the use of edifying, that it may minister grace unto the hearers." (Ephesians 4:29) This, no doubt, is why wise people, in contrast to fools, measure their words and speak less. (Proverbs 17:27-28)

> **James 3:9** Therewith bless we God, even the Father; and therewith curse we men, which are made after the similitude of God. **10** Out of the same mouth proceedeth blessing and cursing. My brethren, these things ought not so to be. **11** Doth a fountain send forth at the same place sweet *water* and bitter? **12** Can the fig tree, my brethren, bear olive berries? either a vine, figs? so *can* no fountain both yield salt water and fresh.

The tongue cannot be controlled because it is corrupted. It is also unnatural. From the same tongue we **bless...God, even the Father**, and then the next moment we **curse...men, which are made after the similitude of God.** All people are made in the image of God. (Genesis 1:26-27, 9:6) That gives humanity a special dignity not true of anything else in creation and has serious implications for how we speak to and about other people. God said to Noah in Genesis 9:6: "Whoso sheddeth man's blood, by man shall his blood be shed: for in the image of God made he man." In the Sermon on the Mount, Jesus explained how the prohibition on murder applies to words spoken in anger and hate:

> **Matthew 5:21** Ye have heard that it was said by them of old time, Thou shalt not kill; and whosoever shall kill shall be in danger of the judgment: **22** But I say unto you,

That whosoever is angry with his brother
without a cause shall be in danger of the
judgment: and whosoever shall say to his
brother, Raca, shall be in danger of the
council: but whosoever shall say, Thou fool,
shall be in danger of hell fire.

James likely has in mind Jesus' words when he relates how
we speak evil of people **made** in the image **of God**. Those
words stand in judgment of the very image **of God**. We
must take this issue seriously because our evil speech
impugns the person **of God**.

Because of our sin nature, **out of the same mouth
proceedeth blessing and cursing**. But as Christian
brethren, these things ought not so to be. Such malicious
speech is contrary to God's design intent for human
language. James illustrates the contradiction against the
divine intent of speech with rhetorical questions. **Doth a
fountain** of water **send forth at the same place sweet
water and bitter** water? A negative answer is required
because a **fountain** is **sweet** or **bitter** by design and cannot
be both. Similarly, **can the fig tree, my** Christian **brethren,
bear olive berries?** Can a **vine** bear **figs?** Of course the
answer is no and no, just as **no fountain both yield salt
water and fresh**.

When our speech is uncontrolled, it becomes a
contradiction out of line with God's design intent. We see
this easily with James' examples from nature, but tend not
to see it in our speech. We self-deceive, convincing
ourselves that if we are "in the right" the words we use do
not matter. I have heard some of the worst speech between
Christians, often on social media, discussing theology or
talking about their pastor or others in their church. And in

the midst of such speech, which on the authority of the book of James affirms their lack of spiritual maturity, those Christians speaking malice and slander to their opponents made in the image **of God** will have the audacity to add that they are "speaking in love." That what you are saying to someone else is the truth, or at least you believe it to be true, does not mean you are speaking in love. Your word choice, tone, the timing of your comments, and to whom you direct your speech, say otherwise. If we are going to learn to tame our speech, we need to be aware of the incongruity in the tongue and how that is contrary to God's will. If we are incapable of controlling our words, we ought to talk less and not compound our sin.

> **James 3:13** Who *is* a wise man and endued with knowledge among you? let him shew out of a good conversation his works with meekness of wisdom. **14** But if ye have bitter envying and strife in your hearts, glory not, and lie not against the truth. **15** This wisdom descendeth not from above, but *is* earthly, sensual, devilish. **16** For where envying and strife *is*, there *is* confusion and every evil work. **17** But the wisdom that is from above is first pure, then peaceable, gentle, *and* easy to be intreated, full of mercy and good fruits, without partiality, and without hypocrisy. **18** And the fruit of righteousness is sown in peace of them that make peace.

James introduces the concept of **wisdom** in the prologue to his epistle in the context of facing the trials of life. The idea of **wisdom** has to do with skill in living. Christians facing trials are encouraged to pray in faith for God's wisdom to aid them in their responses to the trials. (James 1:5-7) The **wisdom** we live by will come out in our speech. There are two kinds of **wisdom** that can guide our lives and our speech. Thus James asks, **who is a wise man and endued with knowledge** (understanding) **among you?** Because the type of wisdom we live by will be reflected in our lives, he says, **let him shew out of a good conversation his works with meekness of wisdom.** In other words, the **wise** Christian should reflect in their **good** conduct **works** done with a **meekness** or humility that derives from their **wisdom**. In this matter of **wisdom**, it is easy to deceive ourselves and mistake worldly **wisdom** for godly or heavenly **wisdom**. We need to know how to tell the difference, and we do so by looking at what it produces in our lives.

James explains that **if ye have bitter envying and strife** or selfishness **in your hearts** (in how you think)**, glory not, and lie not against the truth.** His point is that heavenly **wisdom** will be seen in the humility it produces, but worldly **wisdom** produces the opposite of humility, namely selfish ambition. This heart attitude comes out in our speech in the form of boasting (**glory not**) and lying (**lie not against the truth**). James minces no words about the source of this **wisdom**. It **descendeth not from above**, meaning not from God, but in contrast is **earthly, sensual,** and **devilish** or demonic. Wherever you find **envying and strife**, i.e. selfish ambition among Christians, you find **confusion and every evil work.** Recall earlier how James said evil speech is sourced in "hell." Worldly wisdom is sourced in Satan, fueled by selfish ambition, and produces disorder and **evil** conduct.

Unfortunately, too many Christians live on the basis of worldly **wisdom** and their lives—their thoughts, speech, and actions—reflect it. As Christians we are supposed to learn heavenly **wisdom**. (Proverbs 8; 1 Corinthians 2:6-7; Ephesians 1:17; Colossians 1:9) But too many Christians fail to distinguish the two kinds of **wisdom**, and where they are unaware of God's instruction (or don't care), they fall back on worldly **wisdom** as the basis upon which their decisions and responses are made. Make no mistake about it, if you are not living on the basis of God's **wisdom**, then you are living on and speaking worldly **wisdom**. Moreover, just because you are older or have been around church for a long time does not mean you have God's **wisdom**.

Living on the basis of godly **wisdom** will transform our lives. James explains that **the wisdom that is from above is first pure, then peaceable, gentle, and easy to be intreated** (willing to yield), **full of mercy and good fruits, without partiality, and without hypocrisy.** The word **pure** means without sin or impurity. This is in great contrast to the worldly **wisdom** that produces **every evil work.** Notice that this **wisdom** produces inward changes (**peaceable, gentleness, willing to yield**), as well as outward evidence (**mercy, good fruits**). We cannot help but see that the qualities James wrote of earlier in the context of the coming judgment on believers' works derive from this Godly **wisdom**, including **mercy** (James 2:12-13) and a lack of **partiality** (James 2:1-9).

In fact, living on the basis of heavenly **wisdom** will result in **the fruit of righteousness**, which is **sown** like seeds **in peace of** or by **them that make peace.** Jesus said in the Sermon on the Mount that "blessed are the peacemakers: for they shall be called the children of God." But how do we sow seeds of **peace**? We do so in what we say and do, which are what will be examined in the coming judgment. (James 2:12-13) Connecting the dots, James says that those who control their speech are mature and able to control their entire person. He also says that heavenly **wisdom** produces **righteousness** in our lives so that we become peacemakers rather than those who live to feed our selfish ambition. This kind of living will benefit us at the coming judgment that is not about what we believe but what we speak and do. It is **wisdom** that connects what we know to what we do, and so if our goal is to glorify God then we must rely on heavenly **wisdom**.

Closing

In recent years, news of severe forest fires in the Western United States have become common place. Frequently, the cause is never discovered. But a number of circumstances lead to the devastation, including dry and hot terrains, a spark of ignition, and high winds that fan the flames higher and push them out to burn more land. That is how our speech can be. We don't always realize that the sparks we shoot out of our mouths are finding dry terrain. Once the fire starts, others come to witness the conflagration, not to put out the fire like the thousands who fight the spread of real forest fires, but they join the fray to add their two cents. They add wind to the fire and stoke the wood, but defend their actions as legitimate speech, oblivious or callous to the continuing devastation. It is even worse when someone decides they have the moral high ground as they tend to think that justifies whatever they have to say, however they choose to say it, and the timing and audience of their words. "I am just speaking in love," they might say, as they pour out poison in their words. Forest fires kill people and cause millions of dollars in damages. After hundreds of acres burn, it may take many years before the blackened tree trunks fade away and the green returns, and many decades before the forest returns. Sometimes the land never heals. Many Christians struggle into their elderly years with pains from the past, and often they remember hateful things spoken to them 50 or more years earlier. Children especially remember hateful things their parents said to them. How sad it is if we flippantly say hateful things and those words outlive us and become our legacy. It is far past time that Christians take their speech seriously, reckoning in their hearts that shortly they will answer to Jesus for every idle word.

Application Points

Main Principle: Christians need to control their speech so that their words are rooted in heavenly wisdom and comply with the royal law.

-- There are two types of wisdom, godly wisdom and worldly wisdom, and each is evident in the thinking and behavior it produces.

Discussion Questions

1. Why do you think James says a person that can control his or her speech can control their whole body? (3:2)

2. Does our speech comply with the royal law so long as what we say is true?

3. Why are words so powerful?

4. Are there some practical questions we should ask ourselves before we speak to ensure our speech does not violate the royal law that we love others?

5. What are the differences in attitudes of those that live according to worldly wisdom and those that live according to godly or heavenly wisdom?

6. What are the differences in behaviors of those that live according to worldly wisdom and those that live according to godly or heavenly wisdom?

7. What is the practical significance of knowing that every word we speak will be judged?

Chapter 6

We Need Humility

James 4:1-5:6

In the television series *The Incredible Hulk* that aired from 1977 to 1982, the main character is medical doctor David Banner who did an experiment on himself that went horribly wrong. When he gets angry, he transforms into a larger, muscular, green human with a primitive mind, who is incredibly strong, referred to as the Hulk. When the anger subsides, he transforms back to the brilliant and peaceful Dr. Banner. In a famous line, Dr. Banner says to an irritating news reporter, "Mr. McGee, don't make me angry. You wouldn't like me when I'm angry." Unfortunately, all of us have the ability to go from Dr. Banner to Hulk almost instantly when we get angry. Some Christians talk about righteous anger, like when Jesus cleansed the Temple in John 2, but if we are capable of that I think it rare. We tend to get angry for no better reason than that we are not getting our way. Behind our anger is pride, which tells us we deserve to get our way even if it means others do not get their way. We have rights, and we will vindicate our rights to the highest court in the land, or at least to anyone willing to hear us out and affirm us. We are the hero (or the victim) in all of our stories, the center of our existence. The antidote is humility. Humble people don't have to always get their way, don't have to argue their case all the time, and don't often let the beast within dominate their life and put them at odds with others.

Outline

I. GREETING (1:1)

II. GOD USES TESTS AND TRIALS TO GROW US TO MATURITY (1:1-18)

III. **CENTRAL EXHORTATION:** THE CHRISTIAN GROWING TO MATURITY IS QUICK TO HEAR, SLOW TO SPEAK AND SLOW TO ANGER (1:19-20)

IV. GOOD HEARERS HUMBLY EMBRACE GOD'S IMPLANTED WORD AND LIVE IT OUT TO THE SAVING OF THE SOUL-LIFE AT THE JUDGMENT (1:21-2:26)

V. BE SLOW TO SPEAK BECAUSE YOUR WORDS WILL BE JUDGED AND HOW YOU SPEAK REVEALS YOUR MATURITY AND THE WISDOM YOU LIVE BY (3:1-18)

VI. BE SLOW TO WRATH / ANGER (4:1-5:6)

    a. **Key Principle About Being Slow to Wrath:** Your worldliness causes strife with other Christians and hostility toward God. (4:1-5)

       i. Worldliness causes strife with other Christians. (4:1-2)

    ii. Worldliness ruins your prayer life. (4:2-3)

    iii. A love affair with the world creates hostility with God. (4:4-5)

b. Humble submission to God prevents the negative results of worldliness. (4:6-5:6).

    i. Humility brings us closer to God and He exalts us. (4:6-10)

       1. God gives grace to the humble. (4:6)

       2. Submit to God and resist the devil. (4:7)

       3. Draw near to God with clean hands and pure hearts. (4:8)

       4. Mourn and weep over your sin. (4:9)

       5. Humble yourself before God and He will exalt you. (4:10)

    ii. Humility prevents critical speech toward fellow Christians. (4:11-12)

       1. Critical speech toward fellow Christians makes us judges of the royal law rather than doers of the royal law. (4:11)

       2. Only God has the right to judge. (4:12)

    iii. Humility prevents us from leaving God out of our plans. (4:13-17)

       1. Illustrated by arrogant speech (plans) that leaves God out. (4:13)

       2. Humility recognizes that we are not guaranteed tomorrow. (4:14)

3. Our speech (plans) should reflect our submission to God. (4:15)

4. Boastful speech (plans) is sin. (4:16-17)

iv. Humility prevents us from acting like the wicked rich people who will be judged for oppressing the poor. (5:1-6)

1. The rich oppressors are called upon to mourn their coming judgment. (5:1)

2. Their ill-gotten wealth will stand witness against them. (5:2-4)

3. They lived out worldly desires fattening their hearts for the coming judgment. (5:5)

4. They murdered the righteous who did not resist. (5:6)

Scripture and Comments

Having addressed the matters of being quick to hear and slow to speak, James now addresses anger. He moves beyond outward behavior to the root cause of anger so that he can present a practical solution.

> **James 4:1** From whence *come* wars and fightings among you? *come they* not hence, *even* of your lusts that war in your members? **2** Ye lust, and have not: ye kill, and desire to have, and cannot obtain: ye fight and war, yet ye have not, because ye ask not. **3** Ye ask, and receive not, because ye ask amiss, that ye may consume *it* upon your lusts. **4** Ye adulterers and adulteresses,

> know ye not that the friendship of the
> world is enmity with God? whosoever
> therefore will be a friend of the world is the
> enemy of God. 5 Do ye think that the
> scripture saith in vain, The spirit that
> dwelleth in us lusteth to envy?

James begins the third and final section of the main body
of his epistle. This section expounds on his exhortation to
be "slow to wrath." (James 1:19) He asks the question, **from
whence come wars and fightings among you?** The term
wars is the Greek πόλεμος (polemos) and literally means
war, in the sense of military conflict. (e.g., Matthew 24:6)
But outside the context of military conflict it means "a
state of hostility/antagonism, *strife, conflict, quarrel.*"[49]
The term **fightings** is the Greek μάχη (markē), a term used
"only of battles fought without actual weapons."[50] James'
mix of terms should not surprise us following what he said
about speech in chapter 3. As I previously commented, the
Christian's assault weapon of choice is words. Sadly, most
people that have been in church for several decades have
experienced first-hand what **wars and fightings** look like,
and the cause is rarely doctrinal. Most quarrels happen
over preferences, although in a church context the real
cause of the problem may be dressed in the garbs of a
doctrinal dispute.

James answers his question, explaining that **fightings and
wars...come** from **your lusts that war** or battle **in your
members.** He previously stated: "But every man is tempted,
when he is drawn away of his own **lust**, and enticed. Then
when **lust** hath conceived, it bringeth forth sin: and sin,

---

[49] Ibid., 844.
[50] Ibid., 622.

when it is finished, bringeth forth death." (James 1:14-15) But there James used the Greek term ἐπιθυμία (epithumia), which means a great desire or craving for something forbidden. In the present passage, James uses the term ἡδονή (hēdonē), from which we get the English word "hedonism." The word means a "state or condition of experiencing pleasure for any reason, *pleasure, delight, enjoyment, pleasantness.*"[51] The point here is that their passions battle within their minds and getting what they want for their own pleasure generates conflict. Hodges explains, "James's statement virtually personifies the word *pleasures* so that these *pleasures* become like hostile soldiers who wage *war* within his readers, i.e., *in your* (physical) *members.*"[52] The **war** is between proper passions to honor and serve God and worldly passions for pleasure. We like to say, "so and so made me angry," but that is not Biblical thinking. As Professor Harry Leafe always said, "people and circumstances do not create your spirit, they just help reveal what is already in your heart."

In fact, his readers **lust, and have not.** Ultimately, their problem is worldliness, which James tells us leads to strife with others and hostility toward God. Here, the word **lust** is the Greek ἐπιθυμέω (epithumeō) and is the verb form of the word "lust" used in James 1:14-15. They are fighting among themselves because they lack control of their thought lives. Their passions are in the driver's seat. They crave what they cannot have. In shocking terms, James explains that **ye kill, and desire to have, and cannot obtain: ye fight and war, yet ye have not, because you ask not.** It is doubtful James means they are literally murdering fellow believers, but they

---

[51] Ibid., 434.
[52] Zane C. Hodges, Arthur L. Farstad, and Robert N. Wilkin, *James*, 89–90.

do so in their uncontrolled thinking. (e.g., Matthew 5:22) The description is fitting of undisciplined children who hate those who they perceive as obstacles to their desires. This causes them to **fight**, probably indicating quarrelling (fighting with words not weapons). This also causes them to **war**, suggesting severe hostility.

According to James, they **have not...because ye ask not**. On the one hand, they do not turn to God in prayer for what they actually need. On the other hand, they permit worldliness in their hearts to commandeer their prayer lives. They do not pray for the right things: **ye ask** or pray **and receive not, because ye ask** or pray **amiss, that you may consume it upon your lusts**. The word **lusts** is hēdonē again, meaning pleasures. Their prayers are all about asking God for what they think will allow them the greatest pleasures—the very same pleasures that are the source of their fighting. And God says no. These pleasures set them at war with others and hostility is now between them and God because God will not grant their prayers. The reason is their prayers are not in the will of God like praying for increased ministry opportunities. They are saturated in worldly hedonism so that God indicts them as **adulterers and adulteresses**. James is not speaking of infidelity within their marriages, but infidelity with God—**know ye not that the friendship of the world is enmity with God?** The principle is that **whosoever therefore will be a friend of the world is the enemy of God.**

What a serious charge. They are lovers of the world and not the things of God. Hodges explains this adultery: "Often in the NT, the term *world* (Greek: *kosmos*) is used of a system or entity that is hostile to God and is manipulated by Satan (e.g., 1 Cor 1:20-21; 2:12; Gal 6:14;

2 Pet 1:4; 1 John 2:15–17; 3:1; 5:19). Materialism, immorality, and spiritual blindness are all components of this wicked entity and are in sharp conflict with God's interests and purposes on earth."[53] This is a heart (mind) problem because their desires are bent on selfish pleasures and not godliness, and the hedonistic pursuit of pleasures sets them in conflict with others. Having a love affair with the **world** makes them an **enemy of God**, just as cheating on their spouses would result in hostility within their marriages. That terrible condition means God is not favorably answering their prayers and not blessing them.

James rhetorically asks, **do ye think that the scripture saith in vain, The spirit that dwelleth in us lusteth to envy?** James does not have a specific Old Testament verse in mind. He is saying that they should put two and two together with what the Old Testament says about God's jealousy for His people (**lusteth to envy**) and what the new revelation from God says about His Spirit dwelling in believers (**spirit that dwelleth in us**). The Bible frequently affirms God's jealousy for His own. For instance, "Thus saith the LORD of hosts; I was jealous for Zion with great jealousy, and I was jealous for her with great fury." (Zechariah 8:2) Their love affair with the world sets them at odds with God, who is jealous for His own, and this creates the inner turmoil they are experiencing because God's **spirit...dwelleth in** them, apparently convicting them. This is serious business because **the scripture** does not teach these truths **in vain**.

> **James 4:6** But he giveth more grace. Wherefore he saith, God resisteth the proud, but giveth grace unto the humble.

---

[53] Zane C. Hodges, Arthur L. Farstad, and Robert N. Wilkin, *James*, 93.

Having identified the cause of their going to war with their brethren (being quick to wrath), James identifies the cure with an inclusio on humility. (James 4:6-10) God **giveth more grace.** We need God's **grace** enablement to overcome our internal lusts that "war in [our] members." (James 4:1) It should not surprise us that we need God's resources to overcome our flesh. Paul would later write that we are not only saved (justified) by grace but our sanctification (growth) in our relationship with God is also by grace. (Galatians 3:3) But how do we get **more grace** from God? The principle is that **God resisteth the proud, but giveth grace unto the humble.** The word **humble** is ταπεινός (tapeinos), a term than can refer to a low social status but is also "pertaining to being unpretentious, *humble.*"[54] Recall that James says in his prologue, "Let the brother of low degree rejoice in that he is exalted." (James 1:9) The phrase "low degree" is the same term translated **humble** in this verse. While God resists **the proud,** He exalts (1:9) and **giveth grace** to **the humble** or self-unassuming Christian. Peter emphasizes the same principle using the same Greek term for "humble": "Yea, all *of you* be subject one to another, and be clothed with humility: for God resisteth the proud, and giveth grace to the **humble.**" (1 Peter 5:5) And Jesus employed the same term describing himself: "Take my yoke upon you, and learn of me; for I am meek and **lowly** in heart: and ye shall find rest unto your souls." (Matthew 11:29)

I cannot overstate the importance of the principle that God resists **the proud, but giveth grace unto the humble.** Pride is the most debilitating sin to our Christian walk.

---

[54] William Arndt et al., *A Greek-English Lexicon of the New Testament and Other Early Christian Literature,* 989.

Pride activates our lusts, impacts how we see ourselves and others, prompts our intemperate speech, and fuels our wrath. May I say to those who teach and preach God's Word, and those aspire to, without humility you are not qualified. What James is saying is that **the proud** will lose the war in their members because they will not receive the **grace** they need to overcome. These believers will not grow in **grace** until they first humble themselves. But to the self-unassuming, unpretentious believer, God gives abundantly of His **grace** enablement. We all need that to grow and to avoid being controlled by our anger.

> **James 4:7** Submit yourselves therefore to God. Resist the devil, and he will flee from you.

In light of the principle of James 4:6, the obvious exhortation is to **submit...therefore to God**. Prideful people do not **submit** to God or anyone, although they are often self-deceived by their own pride into believing they are submissive. But the humble do submit, and for that they receive grace. Now by God's grace enablement they can win the war in their members with their own lusts. The writer to Hebrews reminds us that we may "come boldly unto the throne of grace, that we may obtain mercy, and find grace to help in time of need." (Hebrews 4:16) The humble are able to **resist the devil**.

James spends no time building out any doctrine about **the devil**, reflecting his likely belief that his audience knew about Satan's ways. Peter similarly wrote: "Be sober, be vigilant; because your adversary the **devil**, as a roaring lion, walketh about, seeking whom he may devour. Whom resist steadfast in the faith..." (1 Peter 5:8-9) While God wants to renew our minds and radically change us from the inside out so that "the righteousness of God [is] revealed from faith to faith" (Romans 1:17) in our lives, not everyone is on our side. In fact, there is a battle waging for our minds. The war began in the earliest parts of human history when Satan deceived Eve by questioning the veracity of the Word of God: "Yea, hath God said, Ye shall not eat of every tree of the garden?...Ye shall not surely die." (Genesis 3:1, 4) Satan "was a murderer from the beginning, and abode not in the truth, because there is no truth in him." (John 8:44) The apostle Paul warns: "Beware lest any man spoil you through philosophy and vain deceit, after the tradition of men, after the rudiments of the world, and not after Christ." (Colossians 2:8) And again Paul emphasizes: "(For the weapons of our warfare *are* not carnal, but mighty through God to the pulling down of strong holds;) Casting down imaginations, and every high thing that exalteth itself against the knowledge of God, and bringing into captivity every thought to the obedience of Christ." (2 Corinthians 10:4-5)

The primary way **the devil** will go after us is to attack how we think, and as James warns, the source of our problems is our internal lust patterns, i.e., our worldly, hedonistic thinking. Pride makes us easy targets for Satan's deceptions. But the good news is the humble receive grace to successfully **resist the devil** with the assurance that **he will flee from** them.

> **James 4:8** Draw nigh to God, and he will draw nigh to you. Cleanse *your* hands, *ye* sinners; and purify *your* hearts, *ye* double minded.

Again building the principle of humbly submitting themselves to God, James exhorts his readers to **draw**

nigh or near **to God, and he will draw nigh to you.** They are to "resist the devil" so that he flees, but also **draw** near **to God** so that God **will draw** near **to** them. This is a simple but challenging paradigm for living. It is a putting aside of worldly thinking (worldly wisdom, see James 3) and worldly desires in exchange for focusing our affections on the things of **God.** This change must be internal and external, for otherwise we are only hearers of the Word and not doers. (James 1:22-23) Thus James adds, **cleanse your hands, ye sinners.** His Jewish audience understood ceremonial hand washings, but here the point is not literal hand washings but to have "clean hands" in the sense of not being guilty of wrongdoing. That is the external command. But there is also the exhortation to **purify your hearts** or minds, **ye double minded,** for it is in our minds that our lusts reside, the same lusts that give rise to anger and make us easy prey for Satan. That James refers to them as **sinners** and **double** or schizoid **minded** means he sees a serious problem with his audience that needs immediate attention, and the problem is in both their thinking (see the earlier verses on lusts and pride) and their doing (see earlier verses on speech and fighting). They cannot change until they humble themselves, resist the devil and **draw nigh to God.**

> **James 4:9** Be afflicted, and mourn, and weep: let your laughter be turned to mourning, and *your* joy to heaviness.

To change, they need to **be afflicted,** meaning they must acknowledge and grieve their condition. Often the first step in solving a problem is acknowledging the existence and gravity of the problem. In this sin grieving process they should **mourn and weep.** Humility is key because prideful people do not see their faults for which they need to **mourn and weep**. The humble who draw near to God see their sin for what it is and are contrite. They welcome the opportunity for change and growth. We should not live a life of regret, but sincerely acknowledge our condition so we can with God's grace move forward. But James sees his readers gushing over their hedonism and admonishes them to **let your laughter be turned to mourning, and your joy to heaviness**. The sad reality is that many Christians are enjoying their love affair with the world and do not see their own condition, or do not care. They are laughing when they should be **mourning**. There needs to be a brokenness over sin in order for us to grow. Peter writes: "But as he which hath called you is holy, so be ye holy in all manner of conversation." (1 Peter 1:15) As we become more holy we will better see our sin and brokenness and **mourn** it. This reflects that we are overcoming our internal lusts and godly thinking is prevailing in our hearts.

> **James 4:10** Humble yourselves in the sight
> of the Lord, and he shall lift you up.

James completes the inclusio on humility that started in 4:6. There, he wrote, "God resisteth the proud, but giveth grace unto the humble." Now he explains that we should **humble** ourselves **in the sight of the Lord, and he shall lift us up**. James quotes from Proverbs 3:34: "Surely he scorneth the scorners: but he giveth grace unto the lowly." If we don't want to be at enmity with God, and if we want to be able to resist the devil and win the battle within our members, we must humbly submit to God. Then we will get the grace we need for the victorious Christian life and God will **lift** us **up** by enabling our growth and maturity.

We see how this brings us full circle to where James started in his prologue connecting trials to the process of becoming mature. If we want to face the trials of life and grow to maturity, we find the key, the secret weapon if you will, to doing that right here in James 4:10. Sounds easy but humility is that rare gem even among Christians.

> **James 4:11** Speak not evil one of another, brethren. He that speaketh evil of *his* brother, and judgeth his brother, speaketh evil of the law, and judgeth the law: but if thou judge the law, thou art not a doer of the law, but a judge. 12 There is one lawgiver, who is able to save and to destroy: who art thou that judgest another?

We know that humility is the key that unlocks God's grace enablement in our lives so we can draw closer to God rather than giving in to our lusts that war in our members. That same humility is also the key to bridling our speech. James writes, **speak not evil one of another, brethren.** The word **evil** is the Greek καταλαλέω (katalaleō) and means "speak ill of, *speak degradingly of, speak evil of, defame, slander.*"[55] As James repeatedly affirms, he writes to Christian **brethren.** He has in mind Christians disparaging other Christians. James devotes chapter 3 of his epistle to the issue of speech, teaching there that the ability to control our speech is a hallmark of Christian maturity. The warning here is that critical speech runs contrary to the royal **law** of loving others, and in so doing passes judgment on the royal **law** and sets up the Christian critic as a **judge,** usurping God's position. Pride is what makes us judge others, usually in comparison

[55] Ibid., 519.

to our (distorted) view of ourselves. We should never play the comparison game.

James says that **he that speaketh evil** or disparagingly **of his brother, and judgeth his brother, speaketh evil of the law, and judgeth the law.** We need to follow carefully James' chain of thought. In view is **evil**, critical, disparaging or slanderous speech, which **judgeth** or expresses a negative opinion of another person. But at the moment you say those slanderous words and pass judgment on your fellow Christian, you reject not only your fellow Christian but God's royal **law** to love your neighbor as yourself. The royal **law (law** of liberty) is a matter both of how we speak about others and what we do, which is why James says in 2:13: "So speak ye, and so do, as they that shall be judged by the law of liberty." Our unloving speech shows in that moment that we openly despise the royal **law (law** of liberty), and thus we **speaketh evil of the law, and judgeth the law.** But who are we to judge and summarily reject God's royal **law?** When we do that we **art** no longer **a doer of the law** as we should be, **but a judge.**

Once we becomes critics of the royal **law,** we usurp God's role because **there is one lawgiver, who is able to save and to destroy.** Because it is exclusively God's role to be the **lawgiver,** it is exclusively His role to judge **(to save and to destroy).** Thus, James rhetorically asks, **who art thou that judgest another?** In other words, **who** are you that is charged with loving your neighbor to instead judge your neighbor as if you were God? As Paul wrote, "Who art thou that judgest another man's servant? To his own master he standeth or falleth. Yea, he shall be holden up: for God is able to make him stand." (Romans 14:4) We usurp God's role when we judge the royal **law** and when we breach the royal **law** by judging others with our slanderous (**evil**) speech. Behind all of this is pride.

For some reason many Christians cannot connect what James is saying to their own lives. Probably the primary way they deceive themselves is thinking, "if I am right, if I have the moral high ground, my speech and critical treatment of another is justified." I have repeatedly heard Christians say mean spirited things and then protest that they are "speaking the truth in love." Even if you are speaking the truth, and even if you have the moral high ground in some disagreement with another Christian, that is not a license to let your lusts win the war in your members. The empty God-talk that "I said it in love" is as absurd as it is useless when you have to give an account to Jesus.

> **James 4:13** Go to now, ye that say, To day or to morrow we will go into such a city, and continue there a year, and buy and sell, and get gain: **14** Whereas ye know not what *shall be* on the morrow. For what *is* your life? It is even a vapour, that appeareth for a little time, and then vanisheth away. **15** For that ye *ought* to say, If the Lord will, we shall live, and do this, or that. **16** But now ye rejoice in your boastings: all such rejoicing is evil. **17** Therefore to him that knoweth to do good, and doeth *it* not, to him it is sin.

James previously explained that that humility is the key that unlocks God's grace enablement in our lives so that we can draw closer to God rather than giving in to our lusts (4:6-10). He showed that this same humility is the key to controlling our speech (4:11-12). Now he sets out to show how humility prevents us from leaving God out of our plans. James starts this discourse with an illustration of how we articulate plans that leave God out, supposing a hypothetical person with big plans for making money on the basis of his own resources. **Go to now, ye that say, To day or to morrow we will go into such a city, and continue there a year, and buy and sell, and get gain.** First, note that this paragraph (4:13-17) begins with **go to now** just as the next paragraph (5:1-6) will, signaling they are related. The common denominator is materialism. Second, there is debate whether the text should be **or** or "and." As Hodges notes, "The... phrase *today or tomorrow* is read by the majority of the Greek manuscripts of James as *today and tomorrow*, and this is to be preferred."[56] These plans are inherently prideful as 4:16 makes clear. This overconfident person plans in the next two days (**today** and **tomorrow**) to travel to a specific **city**, remain there for **a year**, and conduct a profitable business. None of this is bad in itself. Rather, it is the boastful nature of the plans as articulated that reflect a lack of dependence on God.

James criticizes the overconfident planner, **whereas ye know not what shall be on the morrow.** We take so much for granted in our planning—and I think we all can find ourselves doing this. The planner does not know if they will be alive tomorrow, much less if they will complete the journey. James asks the probing question, **for what is your life?** In the grand scheme of time and eternity it is barely a blip on the screen. James says our life **is even a vapour, that appeareth for a little time, and then vanisheth away.** This is reason to be good stewards of our time, but also to have a healthy concept of our own mortality, which is in God's hands. (Ecclesiastes 7:2-4) Thus our planning should

---

[56] Zane C. Hodges, Arthur L. Farstad, and Robert N. Wilkin, *James*, 100.

be God-oriented, recognizing our complete dependence on Him in all that we do.

James explains how we should plan for the future, addressing the hypothetical overconfident planner of 4:13. **For that ye ought to say, If the Lord will, we shall live, and do this, or that.** I have met Christians that always make a point to say something like "Lord willing." That is not a bad thing, but James' point here is not merely to add some rote verbiage to our speech like "Lord willing" or **if the Lord will.** Rather, it is different paradigm for how we think in our minds that should reflect a complete God-dependence for our next breath, our next day, and our next year. Does our planning issue from our hedonistic lusts that James addressed earlier in the chapter, or is our planning God-oriented? The former type of thinking draws James' criticism, **but now ye rejoice in your boastings: all such rejoicing is evil.** The overconfident planner that leaves God out and rejoices in their well-laid plans is guilty of prideful boasting. This prideful **rejoicing** based on self-sufficiency rather than dependence on God is **evil.** Just as pride leads us to speak critically of others, it also leads us to leave God out of our thinking. We have the ability as Christians to praise God with our lips but live as practical atheists, and this is especially evident in our self-reliance in the area of making money. Humility is the cure because humble people do not boast. Humble people realize their mortality, that their next heartbeat is in God's hands, that tomorrow is God's to give or withhold, and that the success of any venture is ultimately depends on God.

James concludes, **therefore, to him that knoweth to do good, and doeth it not, to him it is sin.** James previously emphasized being a doer of God's Word and not a hearer only. It is not enough to acknowledge our dependence on God. To do that is to know what is right. But our thinking, our plans for the future, and how we express those plans in our speech, must reflect God-dependence. If not, it is boasting and **it is sin**. We need to be a hearer and a doer.

> **James 5:1** Go to now, *ye* rich men, weep and howl for your miseries that shall come upon *you*. **2** Your riches are corrupted, and your garments are motheaten. **3** Your gold and silver is cankered; and the rust of them shall be a witness against you, and shall eat your flesh as it were fire. Ye have heaped treasure together for the last days.

James begins with **go to now** just as he did in 4:13. James emphasizes a concern about his audience's materialism, first in how they show preferential treatment of the wealthy (2:1-3), how they might not share their resources with the poor (2:15-16), how they seek worldly pleasures (4:1-3), and how they focus on the pursuit of money (4:13). In a tone reminiscent of the Old Testament prophets, James now speaks judgment to the **rich** who oppress the poor and trust in their transient wealth. Of course, it is not that he expects those people to receive his letter, but his pronouncement is intended to be understood by his readers as a warning against materialism. Hodges well observes: "His pronouncements are obviously no longer addressed to the Christian community alone, even though the epistle was intended to be read by that community. Yet his words are designed to awaken his readers by means of a crisp announcement about the eschatological doom of all human wealth."[57]

---

[57] Zane C. Hodges, Arthur L. Farstad, and Robert N. Wilkin, *James*, 102.

James says, **go to now, ye rich men, weep and howl for your miseries that shall come upon you.** Judgment is coming upon them because their **riches are corrupted, and their garments are motheaten.** James likely had in mind Jesus' words: "Lay not up for yourselves treasures upon earth, where moth and rust doth corrupt, and where thieves break through and steal: But lay up for yourselves treasures in heaven, where neither moth nor rust doth corrupt, and where thieves do not break through nor steal." (Matthew 6:19-20) These materialistic **rich men** did exactly what Jesus warns against, and their earthly treasure will fade away. In fact, their **gold and silver is cankered; and the rust of them shall be a witness against them, and shall eat** their **flesh as it were fire.** There is a coming judgment and all they will have to show for their lives is their transient wealth, which will burn away. (see also 1 John 2:16-17) They **have heaped treasure together for the last days** when they will face judgment but their **treasure** will not rescue them. Their lives are the fruit of prideful self-sufficiency and, as James will next show, oppressing the poor. The humility James exhorts his audience to will prevent them from acting like the **rich** on whom God pronounces judgment.

> **James 5:4** Behold, the hire of the labourers who have reaped down your fields, which is of you kept back by fraud, crieth: and the cries of them which have reaped are entered into the ears of the Lord of sabaoth. **5** Ye have lived in pleasure on the earth, and been wanton; ye have nourished your hearts, as in a day of slaughter. **6** Ye have condemned *and* killed the just; *and* he doth not resist you.

It is not just that these rich people have bound up their entire lives in their transient wealth, but the manner by which they acquired their wealth is oppressive and in direct violation of the royal law. The reason is that **the hire** or wages **of the labourers who have reaped down their fields** was **kept back by fraud.** They cheated their employees of their pay, and that ill-gotten gain **crieth** out for God's judgment. Likewise, **the cries of them which have reaped** their fields **are entered into the ears of the Lord of Sabaoth,** that is, **the Lord of** armies, against whom their wealth will provide no protection. God hears their cries and will avenge them in the coming judgment. Their oppressors **lived in pleasure** or luxuriously **on the earth, and** have **been wanton** or indulged themselves; they **have nourished** or fattened up their **hearts** for the coming **day of slaughter.** They are the very picture of unbridled hedonism that James warned about in James 4. These rich will not be delivered from the coming judgment because they **have condemned and killed the just** who did **not resist** them. In the end, God will settle the accounts. The message to James' readers is that they should not share the same hedonistic, materialistic motivations or oppress others in violation of the royal law like the rich oppressors who will be judged for their evil works.

Closing

If you google the phrase "anger management," you will find all kinds of definitions and tips to manage your anger. Everyone recognizes this is a problem people struggle with. What you probably will not find is God's antidote to anger problems—humility—which cannot be flipped on like a switch. But even humble people get angry sometimes. So what is a Christian to do when he or she gets angry? The apostle Paul says, "Be ye angry, and sin not: let not the sun go down upon your wrath." (Ephesians 4:26) The fact is that God made us with emotions and Paul recognizes that everyone gets angry. But he is careful to add, "sin not." We make a choice what to do with our anger. On the one hand, we can feed it and let it give way to hostile speech or even violence. This often draws negative responses from others and that stokes our anger more. Alternatively, we can quickly channel the anger in a positive way. This will usually involve pausing and stepping back a moment to reflect before we speak. If our anger is based on what someone else did or failed to do, we can focus on healthy conflict resolution. It is at this point where we again need God's grace enablement to win the battle within our members so that our initial anger stops before it generates sinful speech or behavior. But if in that moment we are bubbling over with pride we will want to vindicate our rights rather than channel our anger. Humility is the way we get the grace we need.

Application Points

Main Principle: The source of conflict with other people is our internal lusts rooted in worldly thinking, but the key to overcoming our lusts is God's grace, which He provides to the humble.

-- God exalts the humble.

-- When we speak evil of another Christian we violate and cast judgment on the other Christian and the royal law, usurping God's sovereign role as judge.

Discussion Questions

1. What is the primary root cause of our conflicts with other people?

2. Can we overcome our sin nature through self-control and personal discipline?

3. When you think of someone that is humble, how would describe their conduct and speech that demonstrates their humility?

4. How does personal conflict with other Christians impact our prayer life?

5. What reasons might a Christian feel free to speak evil of someone else?

6. What is the difference between wise planning for the future and sinful self-reliant planning for the future?

7. What does it look like if a Christian lives like a practical atheist?

8. Can other people make us angry?

Chapter 7

Faithful Endurance

James 5:7-20

In a speech delivered on October 29, 1941 at the Harrow School, in the midst of World War II, Prime Minister Winston Churchill said: "Never give in. Never give in. Never, never, never, never—in nothing, great or small, large or petty—never give in, except to convictions of honour and good sense. Never yield to force. Never yield to the apparently overwhelming might of the enemy." James begins his epistle in the middle of the storm—the trials of life we all face and especially the present trials his readers face. Surmounting these trials lays in the background of the entire epistle and so it is fitting that as James brings his epistle to a close he returns to the issue of endurance. Churchill addressed people in one of the gravest trials of human history, but his words have something for us as well. We cannot quit. We must with God's grace and wisdom endure the storms and run the race set before us. The writer of Hebrews says, "For consider him [Jesus] that endured such contradiction of sinners against himself, lest ye be wearied and faint in your minds." (Hebrews 12:3) And in the same context, he warns to "lay aside every weight, and the sin which doth so easily beset us, and let us run with patience [endurance] the race that is set before us." (Hebrews 12:1) The "sin which doth so easily best us" is quitting—failing to endure, giving in and giving up.

Outline

I. GREETING (1:1)

II. GOD USES TESTS AND TRIALS TO GROW US TO MATURITY (1:1-18)

III. **<u>CENTRAL EXHORTATION</u>**: THE CHRISTIAN GROWING TO MATURITY IS QUICK TO HEAR, SLOW TO SPEAK AND SLOW TO ANGER (1:19-20)

IV. GOOD HEARERS HUMBLY EMBRACE GOD'S IMPLANTED WORD AND LIVE IT OUT TO THE SAVING OF THE SOUL-LIFE AT THE JUDGMENT (1:21-2:26)

V. BE SLOW TO SPEAK BECAUSE YOUR WORDS WILL BE JUDGED AND HOW YOU SPEAK REVEALS YOUR MATURITY AND THE WISDOM YOU LIVE BY (3:1-18)

VI. BE SLOW TO WRATH / ANGER (4:1-5:6)

VII. CLOSING EXHORTATIONS TO ENDURE IN TRIALS KNOWING THE LORD'S RETURN IS NEAR (5:7-11)

    a. Be patient and strengthen your hearts in the knowledge that the Lord's return is near. (5:7-8)

b. Don't fight with fellow Christians because the judge will soon return. (5:9)

c. Illustrated by the prophets who endured through suffering. (5:10)

d. Illustrated by the life of Job, which also shows the Lord's mercy. (5:11)

VIII. CLOSING EXHORTATIONS ON SPEECH (5:12-20)

a. Don't take oaths, but tell the truth. (5:12)

b. The suffering should pray and the merry should sing praises. (5:13)

c. The church elders should anoint and pray over the spiritually weary. (5:14-15)

d. Pray for one another knowing the effectiveness of the prayer of a righteous person. (5:16)

e. Illustrated in the prayers of Elijah. (5:17-18)

f. Share the truth to Christians caught up in false doctrine. (5:19-20)

Scripture and Comments

Having completed the main body of his epistle (1:19-5:6), James provides his final exhortations. These are not unrelated postscripts but practical exhortations based on what was previously written. There is a tendency to read too quickly the final exhortations in our New Testament epistles. But this should be the place where we slow down, reflect, and synthesize how all of the epistle should affect our lives.

> **James 5:7** Be patient therefore, brethren, unto the coming of the Lord. Behold, the husbandman waiteth for the precious fruit of the earth, and hath long patience for it, until he receive the early and latter rain. **8** Be ye also patient; stablish your hearts: for the coming of the Lord draweth nigh.

We must recall that James started with a prologue (1:2-18) about "diverse" trials. While much of the material after the prologue did not specifically refer to trials as such, the subject of trials and storms is the backdrop for everything else in his epistle. The problems of speech, quarrels and pride among his readers is at least partly rooted in how they are failing to properly face their trials. Now, he draws our attention to the trials with the exhortation, **be patient therefore, brethren, unto the coming of the Lord.** The **therefore** looks back to the preceding material, including the immediately preceding material about wealthy people oppressing the poor (5:1-6). The term **patient** is the Greek μακροθυμέω (makrothumeō) and can have the sense of "to remain tranquil while waiting, *have patience, wait*"[58] and but also mean "to bear up under provocation without complaint, *be patient, forbearing.*"[59] The latter better fits the context of trials and oppression, and the point is that they need endurance or "stick-to-it-ness."

James' readers should not lose heart in their trials because **the coming of the Lord draweth nigh** or near. James does not build out any extensive eschatology about the Lord's return, but he obviously assumes both that his audience

---

[58] William Arndt et al., *A Greek-English Lexicon of the New Testament and Other Early Christian Literature*, 612.
[59] Ibid.

believes Jesus will return and has an expectation that will be soon. Some would criticize this as error since nearly 2000 years have passed since the ascension of Christ. But Peter squarely answers this in 2 Peter 3:3-10, where he assures his readers that, "The Lord is not slack concerning his promise, as some men count slackness; but is longsuffering to us-ward, not willing that any should perish, but that all should come to repentance." (2 Peter 3:9) Moreover, our mortal sense of time causes us to misconstrue what it means that the Lord will soon return. As Peter writes, "beloved, be not ignorant of this one thing, that one day *is* with the Lord as a thousand years, and a thousand years as one day." (2 Peter 3:8) God is eternal and not constricted by time.

Every Christian in every time should live with the sure expectation that **the coming of the Lord draweth nigh**. This is the grounding for our ability to patiently endure trials now. Our firm conviction of the veracity of God's promises for the future should cause us to reorient our lives today. That is what it means to have faith in God's Word. (Hebrews 11:1) As Paul says, "For I reckon that the sufferings of this present time *are* not worthy *to be compared* with the glory which shall be revealed in us." (Romans 8:18). It is focusing on all that is associated with the return of Jesus Christ that gives us reason to persevere. James illustrates by calling upon his readers to consider or **behold, the husbandman** or farmer that **waiteth for the precious fruit of the earth, and hath long patience for it, until he receive the early and latter rain.** He waits for the **early and latter rain** which brings the crop or reward for his patience. In the same way, we **also** should be **patient** and **stablish** or strengthen our **hearts** because we know how the story ends. When the Lord returns, accounts will be settled and those who endured faithfully will be rewarded (their soul-lives delivered at the bema per 1:21-2:26 as their faithfulness is rewarded). That is worth waiting for.

> **James 5:9** Grudge not one against another, brethren, lest ye be condemned: behold, the judge standeth before the door. 10 Take, my brethren, the prophets, who have spoken in the name of the Lord, for an example of suffering affliction, and of patience. 11 Behold, we count them happy which endure. Ye have heard of the patience of Job, and have seen the end of the Lord; that the Lord is very pitiful, and of tender mercy.

How we live among our brethren while we wait for Jesus to return is critical. We should not **grudge** or grumble **one against another, brethren, lest ye be condemned** or judged. The word **condemned** is κατακρίνω (katakrinō) and means "pronounce a sentence after determination of guilt, *pronounce a sentence on.*"[60] Some readers automatically assume what is in view in a verse like this is a loss of salvation. But as I showed in the notes on James 1:21-2:26, the judgment at issue is a judgment of believers' works at the bema, and what they stand to gain or lose is rewards *not their eternal life.* James earlier wrote: "So speak ye, and so do, as they that shall be judged by the law of liberty. For he shall have judgment without mercy, that hath shewed no mercy; and mercy rejoiceth against judgment." (James 2:12-13) To grumble against our **brethren** is in direct

---

[60] William Arndt et al., *A Greek-English Lexicon of the New Testament and Other Early Christian Literature*, 519.

violation of the royal law / law of liberty to love our neighbors. James warns the grumbling Christians to **behold, the judge standeth before the door.** This relates to the immediately preceding verse where he says "the coming of the Lord draweth nigh." (James 5:8) The point is that Jesus, **the judge,** will soon return and when he does we will answer for our works at the judgment.

James previously alluded to a farmer to illustrate patience. (James 5:7) He now illustrates the principle with **the prophets, who have spoken in the name of the Lord, for an example of suffering affliction, and of patience.** Those Old Testament **prophets** faithfully preached God's Word to Israel and Judah and were generally persecuted or killed because of it, but they did not back down. Despite their suffering, **we count them happy** or blessed **which endure** through suffering. They are blessed because they endured in hope and God will reward them.

Alluding to a third example, James reminds them of **the patience** or endurance **of Job.** Job was afflicted by Satan but never knew the source or reason for his affliction. Yet he endured and the reader of the book of Job has **seen the end of the Lord; that the Lord is very pitiful** or compassionate **and of tender mercy.** Job lost his children and his possessions, but at the end of the book God restored his riches in abundance and gave him more children. The analogy is that at the bema judgment Jesus will likewise reward those who faithfully endure affliction, and will show mercy to those who are merciful. (James 2:13)

> **James 5:12** But above all things, my brethren, swear not, neither by heaven, neither by the earth, neither by any other oath: but let your yea be yea; and *your* nay, nay; lest ye fall into condemnation.

Continuing his final exhortations, James writes, **above all things**, meaning of chief importance, **my brethren, swear not, neither by heaven, neither by the earth, neither by any other oath**. As he has so frequently done in this short epistle, James returns to the issue of speech. He unquestionably has in mind the words he heard from Jesus:

> **Matthew 5:33** Again, ye have heard that it hath been said by them of old time, Thou shalt not forswear thyself, but shalt perform unto the Lord thine oaths: **34** But I say unto you, Swear not at all; neither by heaven; for it is God's throne: **35** Nor by the earth; for it is his footstool: neither by Jerusalem; for it is the city of the great King. **36** Neither shalt thou swear by thy head, because thou canst not make one hair white or black. **37** But let your communication be, Yea, yea; Nay, nay: for whatsoever is more than these cometh of evil.

When I was a child, sometimes other children (and probably me as well) would "swear on a stack of bibles" and say something like "may lightning strike me if I am lying" as a proof we were being truthful. The implication is that without such oaths, we might be crossing our fingers behind our backs and lying. Jesus calls out this common practice that permitted lying so long as certain oaths were not taken. Jesus' main point is to be truthful in our speech. James says the same, meaning **let your yea be yea; and your nay, nay; lest ye fall into condemnation**. As in James 5:9, James again warns about being judged for our speech at the bema judgment. (cf. James 2:12-14) If we lie, we will answer for it, and we will not be rewarded for that kind of speech. As Jesus elsewhere comments, "every idle word that men shall speak, they shall give account thereof in the day of judgment." (Matthew 12:36) This applies to Christians who are exhorted to "so speak...and so do, as they that shall be judged by the law of liberty." (James 2:12)

Some take this passage and the Matthew 5:33-37 passage to prohibit oaths, for example, as one would be required to do before giving testimony in a court. That misses the point. People should not be left to doubt our truthfulness just because we do not add a vow of truthfulness. It is the abuse of vows as a mechanism to permit untruthfulness that is the offense. For a consistently truthful person to take an oath required by law is no violation.

> **James 5:13** Is any among you afflicted? let him pray. Is any merry? let him sing psalms. **14** Is any sick among you? let him call for the elders of the church; and let them pray over him, anointing him with oil in the name of the Lord: **15** And the prayer of faith shall save the sick, and the Lord shall raise him up; and if he have committed sins, they shall be forgiven him.

We now come to another widely misunderstood passage in this epistle. James asks, **is any among you afflicted?** The word afflicted is the Greek κακοπαθέω (kakopatheō) and means to "suffer misfortune."[61] As previously noted, facing the diverse trials of life is the backdrop for the entire epistle. In the immediate context James exhorts his readers to patient endurance following the examples of the farmer who waits for the rains, the prophets who

---

61 Ibid., 500.

endured affliction, and Job. But we have resources during this time, including especially the privilege of prayer. James simply says, **let him pray.** We may assume this is just a prayer that the affliction will pass, but more likely he has in mind a prayer for God's grace, strength and wisdom. (cf James 1:2-12) Recall his words in 5:8, "be ye also patient; stablish your hearts." James next asks, **is any merry** or in good spirits? That Christian should **sing psalms** or praises to God for His blessings.

James asks, **is any sick among you?** The exhortation is to **let him call for the elders of the church; and let them pray over him, anointing him with oil in the name of the Lord.** The promise is that **the prayer of faith shall** (not may) **save** or deliver **the sick, and the Lord shall raise him up.** The difficulty in this passage is the promise that **the prayer of faith shall save the sick.** I have watched faithful Christians die from horrible diseases like cancers as they and other believers—sometimes thousands of other believers—pray for their deliverance. So what are we to make of this promise? Some teach that this is an absolute promise of physical healing while others, recognizing that faithful Christians die of illnesses, find ways to qualify the promise so that **shall** means "may."

The solution lies in the words translated **sick** in 5:14 and in 5:15, which are different words in the Greek. The term in 5:14 is the Greek ἀσθενέω (astheneō). This word can mean (1) "to suffer a debilitating illness, *be sick*"[62] or (2) "to experience some personal incapacity or limitation, *be weak.*"[63] For the latter, see such verses as 2 Corinthians 12:10 and 13:3 and Romans 14:2. The term **sick** in 5:15 is the

---

[62] Ibid., 142.
[63] Ibid.

Greek κάμνω (kamnō) and has the primary meaning of "be weary, fatigued."[64] We see this this term in verses like Hebrews 12:3 (translated "wearied") and Revelation 2:3 (translated "fainted"). Thus, the term **sick** in 5:14 would include both physical illness as well as weakness or weariness. We may ask, why would someone in this context be so weak or weary that they need prayer from **the elders of the church**. Again, James has trials in mind throughout the epistle, and in the immediate context has affliction in mind (5:13). The exhortation is to faithfully endure trials, but sometimes people grow spiritually weary from the prolonged storms of life. It is to this person— not the physically ill but the spiritually weary—that the promise is made that if **the elders of the church...pray over him, anointing him with oil in the name of the Lord...the prayer of faith shall deliver the** spiritually weak and weary. No doubt, God will give more grace to meet their needs so they may endure.

That this reading is correct is not only supported by the context of afflictions and trials, but also the corollary that **if he have committed sins, they shall be forgiven him.** One reason a Christian may become spiritually wiped out is because they **have committed sins.** While James does not promise healings of all physically ill Christians, he does promise spiritual restoration. The implicit assumption is that this person is not hiding their sins, but has confessed it as sin and stopped. (see James 5:16) This is not unlike what we read in 1 John 1:9 that relates our confession of known sins to a restoration of fellowship. Jesus' blood paid the price for all of our sins, but as we knowingly sin in our daily walk we need to recognize it as sin.

---

64 Ibid., 506.

The **elders of the church**, a likely reference to the leaders (in the formal sense of an elder) but possibly to the more mature, are to anoint their brother or sister **with oil in the name of the Lord**. The word "anoint" is the Greek ἀλείφω (alephō) and means "to anoint by applying a liquid such as oil or perfume, *anoint*."[65] The practice would have been to anoint the **sick** believer with oil (likely olive oil), signifying the presence of God's Holy Spirit with them providing the spiritual restoration. I note that the term "anoint" has been misunderstood and has taken on a life of its own. People refer to a song or a pastor as being "anointed." While these folks are well-meaning, we need to think and speak Biblically. Nowhere does the Bible use the concept of anointed in this way.

> **James 5:16** Confess *your* faults one to another, and pray one for another, that ye may be healed. The effectual fervent prayer of a righteous man availeth much.

Building on what he said about having others pray over the sick, including those that have committed a known sin, James says, **confess your faults one to another**. There is no teaching in the Bible that we are to go to a preacher or priest to "confess" so that he (or she) can mediate between us and God. In 1 John 1:9, the point seems to be that we can speak directly to God in prayer and ask forgiveness for known sins. But we are not to be lone ranger Christians. The New Testament is full of "one another" verses that require us to be around one another to fulfill them. There is great value in developing friendships with other Christians with whom we can speak openly of our struggles and failures and have some

---

[65] Ibid., 41.

accountability. Note in this regard that **faults** can be against other people or against God, and no doubt there is value in confessing both. That requires humility.

Related to being open with (trusted) others about our **faults**, we should **pray one for another, that ye may be healed** or restored. This further confirms the suggested interpretation to James 5:14-15. In relation to our spiritual failings, we can **confess** our **faults** and we can **pray one for another** with the result being restoration. We begin to see how critical all of what James previously wrote becomes. People who cannot control their speech and anger and people that lack humility will not do the things James contemplates in 5:16, and as a result will miss out on blessings. Indeed, **the effectual fervent prayer of a righteous man availeth much**. We should never forget the power of prayer, especially in bringing restoration between two people and between a person and God. The unstated implication is that the **prayer of** the unrighteous Christian **availeth** little.

> **James 5:17** Elias was a man subject to like passions as we are, and he prayed earnestly that it might not rain: and it rained not on the earth by the space of three years and six months. **18** And he prayed again, and the heaven gave rain, and the earth brought forth her fruit.

James illustrates the principle that the "the effectual fervent prayer of a righteous man availeth much." (James 5:16) **Elias** or Elijah, the famous prophet in the Old Testament, **was a man subject to like passions as we are**. We sometimes think the heroes of the faith were more like superheroes of the faith than mortal men and women with faults like ours. But they put their pants on one leg at a time like us and they had faults like us. Elijah exemplifies one who was characteristically righteous. Elijah **prayed earnestly that it might not rain: and it rained not on the earth by the space of three years and six months.** Then **he prayed again, and the heaven gave rain, and the earth brought forth her fruit.** (See 1 Kings 17:1, 18:1) God heard Elijah's prayers and answered them affirmatively. Likewise, the principle is that a **righteous man**, not a perfect man, has the ability affect change through **fervent prayer** just like Elijah. And therefore we should pray for others.

> **James 5:19** Brethren, if any of you do err from the truth, and one convert him; **20** Let him know, that he which converteth the sinner from the error of his way shall save a soul from death, and shall hide a multitude of sins.

In these closing verses, James expresses concern for those caught up in doctrinal error. One last time he addresses his audience as **brethren**, telling them that **if any of you do err from the truth, and one convert him, let him know, that he would convert the sinner from the error of his way shall save a soul from death.** The word **convert** is the Greek ἐπιστρέφω (epistrephō) and means "to return to a point where one has been, *turn around, go back.*"[66] The idea is simply turning one from their wrong doctrine back to sound apostolic doctrine. (cf. 2 Timothy 2:24-26; Jude 22-23) We should not read **soul** to mean "spirit." We have already encountered this term in James 1:21: "Wherefore lay apart all filthiness and superfluity of naughtiness, and

---

[66] Ibid., 382.

receive with meekness the engrafted word, which is able to save your souls." If receiving God's Word in humility is able to "save" or deliver our "souls," it stands to reason that sound doctrine is critical to the Christian walk. False doctrine is not "able to save your souls" and may lead you to despair and ruin.

Not all errors in doctrine have the same significance. I think we can be mistaken about some doctrinal matters without it throwing our life off course. I hasten to add that no one has all of their doctrinal ducks in a row. We all have blind spots in our theology. But that said, there are some false doctrines that are particularly destructive and cause what James calls **death**. As an example, the entire book of Galatians was written to address the false doctrine that Christians must keep the Law of Moses to be Christians and grow as Christians, and the apostle Paul minced no words about this deadly doctrinal error.

James says that turning someone from their **error** is able to **save a soul from death**. Of course, **error** may lead to physical death as we face the consequences of bad choices or receive divine discipline. But we have an antecedent for **death** in James 1:15: "Then when lust hath conceived, it bringeth forth sin: and sin, when it is finished, bringeth forth death." In contrast to those that endure trials in faithful reliance on God's Word and receive the "crown of life" (James 1:12), those that get snared in bad doctrine will sin (James calls this person **the sinner**) and experience **death** in their daily walk. This indicates an absence of fellowship with Jesus and personal ruin. This should not surprise us given the immediate context of those who are sick and need restoration and forgiveness of their sins. (James 5:14-15)

Finally, James adds, **and shall hide** or cover **a multitude of sins**. James envisions someone tangled in bad doctrine that causes them to sin and experience **death** in their walk. It stands to reason that if they can be turned back to the truth, those new sin issues that derive from their aberrant doctrine will go away. God's Word is able to **save a soul** but false teaching will do the opposite. It will destroy a soul-life by leading to a life of ruin that is harshly judged by Christ at the bema and no rewards are given. We need to be available to help in the restoration of our brethren, for this fulfills the royal law and will be rewarded at the bema judgment. On this point, we do well to consider Paul's words to Timothy about how to try to help those caught up in error:

> **2 Timothy 2:24** And the servant of the Lord must not strive; but be gentle unto all *men*, apt to teach, patient, **25** In meekness instructing those that oppose themselves; if God peradventure will give them repentance to the acknowledging of the truth; **26** And *that* they may recover themselves out of the snare of the devil, who are taken captive by him at his will.

What Paul says is that we have to approach people caught up in destructive doctrine with great care and a humble spirit. That should sound familiar given James' emphasis on humility. I would suggest humble Christians are far less likely get caught up in deadly error. Paul says God "peradventure," that is He might give them "repentance," meaning a change of thinking from bad doctrine back to apostolic doctrine. But note that Paul says these folks have been snared like an animal in a trap by Satan and will be used by Satan to do Satan's will. That is why people caught up in deadly doctrines are so aggressive to find and victimize others with their newfound ideas. The royal law requires that we try to help, but wisely and humbly so we avoid the snare of the devil ourselves.

Closing

I said at the beginning of this study that James is an easy book but widely misunderstood because people have theological commitments that blind them to what James has to say. As we synthesize the entire epistle, we understand that our Christian lives will be a series of tests and trials that range from minor matters that we may not even consider a trial to major storms with finances, health, and relationships. God doesn't take all the trials away, but He uses them to grow us, to teach us endurance as we move to maturity. Because we cannot do what we do not know, we must make learning God's Word (humbly embracing the implanted word) our priority. But it is no mere academic matter. We are to learn God's Word experientially as we live and apply it in our trials. In one way or another, every violation in the Bible is a violation of the royal law to love God and love others. This is why James focuses on the royal law, which no one can claim to not understand. God gives us His Word, His wisdom, and His grace to endure trials and love people along the way. A Christian life well-lived is one that characteristically loves God and others. The world and the devil would distract us and try to get our priorities mixed up. We are going to be rich toward God or toward the world. Those rich toward God are laying up treasure in heaven and at the coming judgment of their soul-lives will be rewarded by Jesus. That is what the saving of the soul is all about. Going to heaven is not getting halos and harps. Life is serious business.

Application Points

Main Principle: Christians need to endure the trials of life with humility like the prophets and like Job.

-- When we are spiritually spent, especially if we have continued in an area of sin, we need to seek restoration in prayer and with the prayers of others.

-- We have a responsibility (royal law obligation) for the physical and spiritual well-being of others within our sphere of influence, and should help as we are able with those caught up in destructive false doctrine.

Discussion Questions

1. What is endurance in our Christian walk? What is it not?

2. Does James prohibit all oaths and vows? Consider the oath / vow taken in a court before offering testimony, between a man and woman in a wedding ceremony, the oath / vow taken as one enters certain professions (law, medicine, police officer, fireman), etc.

3. Does James promise that physically sick people will always be healed through prayer? Does the Bible promise that?

4. How is the concept of being anointed used in the book of James? In the Bible? Are there ways Christians commonly use the concept of anointed or anointing that had no basis in the Bible?

5. Does James 5:16 teach that we must confess our sins regularly to a preacher or priest?

About the Author

HUTSON SMELLEY resides in Chappell Hill, Texas with his wife and children. He holds advanced degrees in mathematics, law and Biblical studies, and is an adjunct professor at the College of Biblical Studies. He can be contacted at: proclaimtheword@mac.com

www.proclaimtheword.me

www.ingramcontent.com/pod-product-compliance
Lightning Source LLC
Chambersburg PA
CBHW071856020426
42331CB00010B/2534